PERSONAL DEVELOPMENT MATTERS

A guide and step-by-step educational workbook for helping young people aged roughly 11-16 with complex needs to get to know themselves better

Kathryn Plant

meadows
Building a future for young people

Russell House Publishing

First published in 2011 by:
Russell House Publishing Ltd.
Temple House
57/58 Broad Street
Lyme Regis
Dorset DT7 3QF
Tel: 01297-443948
Fax: 01297-442722
e-mail: help@russellhouse.co.uk
www.russellhouse.co.uk

British Library Cataloguing-in-publication Data:
A catalogue record for this book is available from the British Library.
ISBN: 978-1-905541-69-0

Typeset by Jeremy Spencer
Section page illustrations by Andrew Hill; pages 15, 39, 57, 100, 110 from fotolia.com
Photographs on pages 70-77 from istockphoto.com
Printed by IQ Laser Press, Aldershot

Russell House Publishing
…aims to publish innovative and valuable materials to help managers, practitioners, trainers, educators and students.

Our full catalogue covers:
social policy, working with young people, helping children and families, care of older people, social care, combating social exclusion, revitalising communities and working with offenders.

Full details can be found at www.russellhouse.co.uk
and we are pleased to send out information to you by post.

Our contact details are on this page.

We are always keen to receive feedback on publications and new ideas for future projects.

Contents

Why does *My Personal Development Workbook* exist?

My teaching experience has been gained in England but I believe those working in Scotland, Wales and Northern Ireland should find this workbook is just as relevant as it doesn't contain anything that ties it culturally or legally to England alone.

Whilst working as a teacher for Meadowcare (a residential childcare company) I was given the job of coordinating and teaching Personal, Social, Health and Citizenship Education (PSHCE). The company provided residential care and 1:1 education and therapy as all the young people had complex needs – many having statements of special educational needs (SEN). Most of the young people had challenging behaviour and had experienced significant trauma from childhood.

As part of my professional development I had gained a Level 3 qualification in counselling skills and had a keen interest in the therapeutic services that the company offered. As a firm believer of SEAL, and as the initiative was being implemented at the time into all schools, I decided along with the senior management team to implement it into our education service to keep in line with mainstream schools.

For those who are unfamiliar with SEAL – Social and Emotional Aspects of Learning (DCSF, 2005) the Department for Children, Schools and Families produced materials to be used as a curriculum resource as a result of the National Strategies Behaviour and Attendance pilot. This resource aims to develop the underpinning qualities and skills that help promote positive behaviour and effective learning.

Although the resources provided by the DCSF are comprehensive, I felt they were designed for use predominantly in mainstream schools. Whilst trying to implement the SEAL resources in a residential childcare setting I was faced with two problems. The first being that I didn't have a class to work with, most of the SEAL resources are designed for group work and the policy at my organisation was to work with young people on a one to one basis. The second was that some of the resources available were inappropriate for the looked after children that I worked with. I felt the resources appeared to assume that each young person lived in a family home and experienced only typical traumas. As this was not the case for the young people I worked with, I found myself using only small sections of material that I felt would benefit them. As lots of publications are available on the market about feelings and self-esteem I began to build up a collection. Using small sections of each resource that I felt were appropriate for my students; I spent time putting together a programme that was suitable, incorporating elements of the SEAL resource. This task was extremely time consuming and it was often necessary to adapt material or worksheets to make them more suitable, as I felt that it was important to deliver a programme that ran smoothly and felt coherent to the young people.

Eventually I decided to stop focusing on adapting existing resources and searching for something that I felt I would never find. I decided to write my own resource specifically for young people with complex needs that addressed all the important issues that, in my experience, were crucial to their personal development.

From the outset I wanted the resource to contain the essence of SEAL as I still felt that the social and emotional skills underpin effective learning. However, I also wanted the resource to be a chance for each looked after young person to begin a journey of personal development and self-awareness to enhance their ability to learn effectively, become more resilient and to strengthen their existing positive qualities. My aim was to let the workbook allow young people to speak honestly about their unique experience of being in the care system, and explore their feelings around the relationships they feel have been affected.

I also wanted the workbook to enhance the young person's understandings of their own emotions not only by expanding their vocabulary, but by understanding their own triggers and the biological factors behind some of their behaviours. The facilitator of the workbook encourages the young person to play an active role in the learning, and this philosophy aims to empower them to build on their self-confidence and learn a variety of skills to aid their own personal development. I have taught the workbook to a number of young people on a one to one basis and I have found it to be an invaluable tool. Although every young person is different and the depth at which they engage is variable, it has greatly enhanced the self-awareness of each young person that has worked through it.

I used the workbook as a teaching resource and it was on the timetable as PSHCE. I was observed by an Ofsted inspector in January 2010 whilst facilitating the workbook and he took the time to look over it in detail. The feedback I was given was extremely positive and he found it very encouraging that such a resource was being used during education with young people who had differing complex needs.

Each young person I taught also received therapy once each week. I was able to forge strong links with the therapists and discuss the content of the sessions. This provided them with an insight into the themes on which we were working.

The young people took ownership of their workbook and liked to include pictures and other personal material when given the option. The feedback I received from the young people was very positive: they all reported that it had helped them in many different ways. The results of the strengths and difficulties questionnaire which we used to measure the effectiveness of the workbook along with the therapy sessions the young person received all showed a marked improvement in how the young person was able to cope with different situations.

I have explored the delivery of the workbook by other professionals including therapists, psychologists and staff involved in the youth justice system. The feedback was so positive that it formed my opinion that the workbook should be available to a variety of professionals involved with young people, not just to the professionals who are involved with looked after young people.

I, along with other members of staff at the same company, continue to use the workbook with young people.

Kathryn Plant, 2011

Introduction

Who this book is for

My Personal Development Workbook is a comprehensive educational programme of personal and emotional development designed principally for work, either in or out of education time, with 11-16 year olds:

- Who are **looked after**.
- Who have **complex needs** and who are receiving support and intervention from professionals.
- Who have **special educational needs** (SEN) including those who have statements, whose targets include improving behaviour, increasing self-esteem and expressing emotions more appropriately.
- Other young people in any of the above contexts with the intention of beginning **life story work** at a later date.

In some instances the workbook might be used with young people, in any of these contexts, who are somewhat older or younger.

What is *My Personal Development Workbook*?

The workbook, which is reproduced in full in this manual, starting on page 1, covers five main areas:

- All about Me.
- My feelings.
- My behaviour.
- My relationships.
- My self-esteem and confidence.

and finally a summary.

The workbook has been written in such a way that the first section concentrates on safe exploration tasks and activities that help to forge a positive and trusting relationship between the facilitator and the young person. As the sections progress and the relationship develops the material begins to explore more difficult issues. The programme is designed to build on the learning, section by section. But, just as effectively, the separate sections can be used independently to address the specific needs of young people, rather than as part of the book's overall programme.

The workbook was originally developed for use in a residential child care setting where the author found that the government-developed material for teaching the *Social and Emotional Aspects of Learning (SEAL)* needed significant adaptation and development for her work in these one-to-one settings.

The *SEAL* resources appeared to assume that each young person lived at home with a family who cared for them and experienced only the typical traumas that most young people experience such as a grandparent or pet dying. They also seem to assume that all young people have similar needs at the various stages of their lives. This workbook addresses the typical circumstances: but then it goes on to try and help young people deal with things that may *not* be typical.

Although the workbook has a therapeutic dimension it is an educational tool, not therapy. When being used in a therapeutic capacity by psychologists, therapists and counsellors it is an alternative intervention similar to other intervention publications on the market.

It is principally designed for delivery on a one to one basis for one hour per week, over the course of a year. It can also be taught in a small group setting by facilitators who are comfortable with the extra demands of group work with these young people.

Following the recent change of government their plans are for *Social and Emotional Aspects of Learning* are uncertain. At the time this workbook went to press there was no current information regarding any changes to *SEAL* on the new Department for Education website **www.education.gov.uk**. Over £10 million was invested in the development of *SEAL* and it has been implemented in the majority of schools across the country. If changes do take place there will need to be something equivalent to *SEAL* which has now become embedded in many school curriculums. To change it radically would disrupt the current teaching climate and an extended period of transition would be necessary. However, it seems unlikely that it would be removed altogether.

Who can deliver the workbook?

- Teachers and learning mentors.
- Psychologists, therapists and counsellors.
- Professionals involved in the youth justice service.
- Social workers, residential social workers, key workers.
- Foster carers.

The list of suggested facilitators above is not exhaustive. Other professionals involved in long-term interventions with young people may use it, for example, health professionals in a mental health unit or family workers supporting young people within their own homes or Connexions workers.

In all of these contexts the workbook also supports and contributes to the *Every Child Matters* agenda which strives to change and improve outcomes for children and young people.

Regardless of their profession, the role of the facilitator is critical to the effectiveness of the workbook.

Skills taught and developed during the *My Personal Development Workbook* programme

The skills taught and practised during the workbook enable the young person to:

- Identify healthy and positive relationships
- Gain a better understanding of difficult relationships
- Identify abusive behaviour
- Enhance coping skills and resilience
- Enhance own empathy
- Increase optimism
- Identify rewards
- Identify positive role models
- Explore own feelings
- Manage expression of emotion more appropriately
- Enhance awareness of body cues
- Use positive self talk
- Protect and support self
- Minimise harm in risky situations
- Explore body image
- Explore personal values
- Identify prejudice and discrimination
- Enhance understanding of their own and others behaviour
- Enhance communication skills
- Recognise personal qualities

About the author

Kathryn Plant has ten years experience teaching young people who have challenging behaviour and complex needs. She has spent the last five years working with vulnerable looked after young people at Meadows Care (www.meadowscare.co.uk) and has a passion for helping them to develop healthy self-esteem.

Comments from professionals who have used the workbook

I have now used the workbook with a number of young, looked-after children. I have found it to be an excellent tool for engaging young people, for discussing personal topics in a safe and enjoyable way and for guiding a young person through exercises and tasks to develop their self-awareness. The workbook can be completed at any pace, according to the emotional needs and development level of the person you are working with, which makes it a very flexible and adaptable tool, open to a full range of young people. I have been able to utilise the workbook in a number of different ways. I used the workbook with one young person who was very against specific therapy but was happy to use the workbook within the context of PSHCE. Whilst working through the first section, trust and rapport began to develop, which then led the young person to request therapeutic work in addition to the workbook. Another young person who had grown apprehensive and fearful of therapy and therapists felt comfortable enough to complete the workbook. By focusing in on certain sections we were able to complete some beneficial work and increase her emotional awareness and understanding of herself: she also had a different and more positive attitude to talking about herself and about personal issues. This will undoubtedly benefit her in the long term.

Dr Jane Toner – Clinical Psychologist

As a teacher of PSHCE working with very vulnerable young people, I have found the workbook an extremely valuable tool. The workbook's foundation in the SEAL (social and emotional aspects of learning) approach guides students in a logical manner through the five key aspects of social and emotional learning – self awareness, managing feelings, motivation, empathy and social skills. I have found that the workbook's conversational friendly script, illustrations, and clear-cut activities motivate the young person to actively participate in and often direct their own learning. The schemes of work that are included offer straightforward assistance to the adult 'coach' leading the sessions. Though I am not a trained PSHCE teacher and have not been teaching it a long time, I have felt confident using this resource and have already seen noticeable improvements in our young people's self-awareness and understanding of their own emotions.

Liva Hansen – Teacher

I have found the workbook helpful and constructive in aiding therapeutic interventions. From an educational therapeutic perspective it provides a comprehensive and structured way to assist young people with complex psychological needs to begin learning about themselves in a more fun and safe way. Therapeutically it allows the young person to begin understanding emotional difficulty by supporting the development of a formulation-based approach to therapy. I have used the workbook and found it helpful in engaging young people with emotional problems and assisting them to socialise to models of emotional disorders: the chapters incorporating emotions and behaviour have been particularly helpful for this reason. The breadth of the topics included and the structure means I have been able to tailor it: using it both systematically and as individual modules. The layout and exercises included have made difficult engagement work easier for young people, more fun and engaging whilst giving me options I would not have considered using previously. Completing these sections with young people has enabled me to identify important themes for future work, whilst considering where my work sits in relation to wider emotional education needs of young people and how developing an understanding of themselves is important.

Simon Lynch – Cognitive Behavioural Therapist

Copying permission for the manual

Purchasers of **Personal Development Matters** are allowed to undertake incidental photocopying from it for use in training, and for when working at various times with any individual young person on just two or three pages to meet specific needs that arise.

If you want to make multiple copies of a few pages, please check whether that is permitted under your licence with the Copyright Licencing Agency, if you have one. If you are uncertain about this, you must seek permission from the publisher at help@russellhouse. co.uk or on 01297 443948.

No copied material may be resold.

Discount purchase of the loose-leaf sets of the workbook

This manual, *Personal Development Matters*, includes the 183 pages that comprise **My Personal Development Workbook: a step-by-step workbook for getting to know myself better**. See pages 1 to 183.

When you are doing anything more than incidental work with young people, you will need to purchase a copy of *My Personal Development Workbook* for each of them, so that they can work with their own copy over time.

To help with this, **looseleaf hole-punched** versions of the workbook and its cover are **only available direct from the publisher** at **significant discounts**.

The publisher can give you the latest prices, etc for the looseleaf versions. At the time of publication, a single copy carries the same price as the complete manual. Discount rates start at 2 copies. The unit price for 10 or more copies is less than 50% of the single-copy price.

For full information contact the publisher on help@russellhouse.co.uk or on 01297 443948.

This material in *My Personal Development Workbook* is only available in hard copy. It may not be digitised, copied or resold under any circumstances.

Summary of the skills needed for effective facilitation

It is important that the facilitator has experience communicating with young people and feels confident that they are able to deliver a programme of this nature. No formal qualifications are required to deliver the workbook but a qualification or experience in counselling skills would be an advantage, as it would enhance the facilitator's skills of supporting and responding. At the very least being competent in the skills outlined below is essential.

Empathy

During the delivery of the workbook empathy is an essential skill as it plays a major role in building a positive relationship with the young person and impacts greatly on the effectiveness of the workbook. Active listening is an integral part of conveying empathy: it is listening with the intent to hear the meaning behind the words and is a structured way of listening to others. It is important that the facilitator can harness the skill of conveying empathy as part of the discussion work throughout all sections of the workbook.

Reflection

During discussion work, reflecting back to young people what they have just said can be a way to communicate acceptance and clarify that you have understood. It also conveys empathy and a sense that you are really listening. It is important to use the skill of reflecting back appropriately, as simply sounding like a parrot will not help to forge a good relationship at all.

Paraphrasing

Paraphrasing should be used during discussion work. Stating in your own words what the young person has just said can help clarify what they are saying and gives you the opportunity to check your understanding, and the accuracy of your perception. It can also provide a pause in the session and allow you both to reflect and think.

Summarising

Summarising is an important skill to have, as you need to be able to tie together multiple elements of what the young person has talked about during the session. It's also important to use a summary at the end of the session to recap the material covered.

The schemes of work

The schemes of work for each of the areas is shown on the next few pages.

Scheme of work　　　　　　　　Young person or group _____

Section 1 All about ME　　　　　Coach _____

Objective	Activity	Resources	Learning Outcome
Introduction – begin to build relationship.	• Complete the 'Getting to know you questionnaire'.	workbook, pen	• Young person and coach have hopefully begun to build rapport.
To enhance personal awareness.	• Get the measure of me exercise, draw around the outline of young person and work through the instructions. • What my body can do exercise.	tape measure, long roll of paper, felt tips stop watch, workbook photo of young person	• Young person begins to explore their physical self and gains a better understanding of what their bodies can do.
To enhance personal awareness of the young person's social life.	• Social me – fill in questionnaire.	workbook, pen	• Young person begins to explore their social life and looks at particular aspects in more detail.
To identify all the people that the young person feels they have a relationship with and place them in context on the social circle.	• Social me – construct the young persons social circle using the provided template.	workbook, pen	• Using the constructed circle the young person can appreciate a visual representation of the people they have contact with and the relationship they have with each person.
To identify the social settings that the young person attends and reflect on the pros and cons of being placed in their current care provision.	• Social me – complete the social environments questionnaire. • Fill in the table of gains and losses.	workbook, pen	• Young person identifies all the social settings they attend and begins to link experiences and feelings to three chosen settings. • Begin to identify the gains and losses of their social life since being placed at current provision.
Reflect on the changes to their social life and summarise what those changes mean to them.	• Social me – summary of social me.	workbook, pen	• Summarise the main aspects of their own social life.
Reflect on the work covered in the section 'social me'.	• Social me – complete the worksheet 'time to think'.	workbook, pen, art materials	• Recognise the main learning points from this section of the workbook.
Young person begins to explore their cultural heritage.	• My culture – complete the cultural questionnaire.	workbook, pen	• Young person can identify basic cultural information they feel belongs to them.　　→

G12

Objective	Activity	Resources	Learning Outcome
Identify own cultural role models and show awareness of youth culture and how it affects them.	• My culture – look at different cultural role models and discuss youth culture.	workbook, pen	• Identify own cultural role models and explain why.
Identify the meaning of prejudice and explore how the young person feels about prejudice.	• My culture – identify other cultures and the barriers that different cultures have to face. • Explore prejudice and the reasons why it exists linking it to their own experiences.	workbook, pen	• Conclude why prejudice exists and explore their own feelings around prejudice.
Reflect on the work covered in this section 'my culture'.	• My culture – complete the worksheet 'time to think'.	workbook, pen, art materials	• Recognise the main learning points from this section of the workbook.
Explore the meaning of image and raise awareness of the different youth groups that exist. Explore the young persons feelings about each group.	• My image – explore different groups of image including emo's, chav's, hoodies etc. • Complete research on the internet and produce an A4 page for each.	workbook, pen, PC, internet access, printer	• Identify the key components for each group and explore what they think about each group.
Explore the young persons image and identify key or consistent aspects of their own image.	• My image – complete the worksheets exploring own image.	workbook, pen	• Identify the young persons own image and give it a name if the young person does not feel they belong to any of the researched groups.
Reflect on the work covered in this section 'my image'.	• My image – complete the worksheet 'time to think'.	workbook, pen art materials	• Recoginse the main learning points from this section of the workbook.
Explore the young persons value base.	• My values – complete the task rating what is important to the young person.	workbook, pen	• Identify from the choices given where the young persons values lie, discuss what might influence these values.
Explore the young persons value base.	• My values – complete the values table. Photocopy then cut out the statements and glue each one in the column the young person feels it belongs and discuss why.	workbook, pen, scissors, glue, photocopy	• Using the table try to identify a pattern and pick out themes in the young persons value base to increase self awareness.
Identify a role model and explore if their values are something that influence the young person.	• My values – identify a person that the young person looks up to and explore what you think their values might be.	workbook, pen	• Conclude if there is a link between a role model and their value base.

→

Objective	Activity	Resources	Learning Outcome
Develop a set of life rules based on the information revealed in this section.	• My values – write a set of life rules.	workbook, pen	• Develop a set of life rules based on the personal values of the young person.
Reflect on the work covered in this section 'my values'.	• My values – complete the worksheet 'time to think'.	workbook, pen, art materials	• Recognise the main learning points from this section of the workbook.
Begin to raise self awareness in the young person by identifying particular strengths and weaknesses.	• Raising self-awareness – complete the questions and discuss each answer.	workbook, pen	• Recognise own strengths, weaknesses and achievement.
Explore what makes the young person feel happy, confused, upset and angry.	• Raising self-awareness – complete the started sentences.	workbook, pen	• Link a situation to the feelings in each sentence.
Recognise own positive qualities.	• Raising self-awareness – from the list provided circle the positive qualities the young person feels they possess.	workbook, pen	• Identify their own positive qualities and begin to explore what they have to offer.
Reflect on the work covered in this section 'my values'.	• Raising self-awareness – complete the worksheet 'time to think'.	workbook, pen, art materials	• Recognise the main learning points from this section of the workbook.
Begin to explore the young persons personality.	• My personality – access the internet and website; www.bbc.uk/science/human body • Complete the tests stated in the workbook and print out the results.	workbook, PC, internet access printer	• Conclude from the results of the experiments what type of personality they have.
Identify the different ways in which people can be intelligent and complete the multiple intelligence test.	• My personality – access the internet and website; www.bgfl.org • Complete the multiple intelligence test and print out the results.	workbook, PC, internet access, printer	• Conclude from the multiple intelligence test, which kind of intelligence is their strength.
Identify different parts of their own personality comparing it with the perception of a member of staff.	• My personality – complete the personality questions and answer on a scale of 1-10.	workbook, pen, member of staff	• Compare the answers of the young person with the answers from the member of staff.

→

Objective	Activity	Resources	Learning Outcome
Complete a comprehensive breakdown of the young persons personality using all the information just gathered.	• My personality – complete the personality wall putting the largest parts of the personality at the bottom for the foundation working up.	workbook, pen	• Determine what different attributes make up the young persons personality.
Reflect on the work covered in this section 'my personality'.	• My personality – complete the worksheet 'time to think'.	workbook, pen, art materials	• Recoginse the main learning points from this section of the workbook.
Identify all the locations connected to the young person from an aerial viewpoint and print out.	• My place in the world – access the internet and Google earth and print out all the geographical locations the young person has. • On the map of the British Isles label all the connections the young person has and write on distances to their current location.	workbook, pen PC, internet access, printer workbook, pen	• Use Google earth to locate various places and addresses and collate all the information to show geographical connections. • Show geographical connections on a map of the British isles.
Young person is able to appreciate a visual 3D representation of where they fit in the world and how they are connected to different towns, places and countries.	• My place in the world – make a papier mâché globe together and once dry paint. Mark on all the global connections that the young person has with a felt tip including family connections, music, favourite food etc.	flour, water, newspaper, balloon, paint	• Identify all the global connections that the young person has.
Devise a family tree.	• My place in the world – complete a family tree on the page provided.	workbook, pen	• Construct a family tree and be able to show all the different family connections.
Reflect on the work covered in this section 'my place in the world'.	• My place in the world – complete the worksheet 'time to think'.	workbook, pen, art materials	• Recoginse the main learning points from this section of the workbook.

Scheme of work
Section 2 My feelings

Young person or group _____

Coach _____

Objective	Activity	Resources	Learning Outcome
Introduction – understand the dictionary meaning of 'feelings'. Begin to explore basic feelings when prompted by a scenario.	• Look up the meaning of 'feelings' and discuss. • Finish the statement 'Exercise…'	dictionary, workbook, pen	• Describe what is meant by feelings and identify their own basic feelings when prompted by the scenarios.
Explore facial expression and body language linked to various emotions.	• Feelings bingo – guess the feeling whilst playing bingo, involve another staff member to make the game last longer.	feelings bingo game, photocopy	• Identify or interpret feelings from seeing facial expression and body language.
Understand what is meant by non-verbal communication and how important it is in different situations.	• Read through the non-verbal communication section together and discuss.	workbook, pen, Feelings images	• Recognise the importance of non-verbal communication and show understanding of appropriate body language for different situations.
Understand that feeling confident can be difficult.	• Explore a time when the young person felt confident.	workbook, pen	• Identify what it is like to feel confident and relate it to personal experience.
Enhance the young persons vocabulary for a variety of emotions, use a dictionary for any words that the young person does not know the meaning for.	• Select each feeling and put it into one of four basic categories then discuss.	workbook, pen	• Expand the young persons vocabulary for feelings.
Explore the frequency of their own feelings and begin to explore what is physically going on when they experience particular feelings.	• Young person is to rate their own emotional profile and explore a chosen feeling by annotating on the body diagram.	workbook, pen	• The young person should begin to feel more self aware about their emotions and understand that their body responds to emotions in a physical way e.g. sweating palms.
The young person begins to explore more complex feelings when prompted by a scenario.	• Read 'tricky feelings' together and discuss. • Finish the statements exercise.	workbook, pen	• Define their own feelings by using the vocabulary from previous sessions when prompted by the scenarios.
Recognise that sharing feelings can be beneficial and identify what qualities the listener needs to have for the sharing to be a positive experience.	• Read 'sharing feelings' together and discuss. The young person is to identify someone that they feel comfortable sharing their feelings with and why.	workbook, pen, photocopy	• Understand the importance of sharing feelings with a person they feel safe with. →

Objective	Activity	Resources	Learning Outcome
Understand what is meant by 'empathy' and being 'empathetic'.	• Read through empathy together and discuss. Look back over previous work to find evidence of empathy. • Young person is to design a poster to promote empathy.	workbook, pen, PC, art materials, Feelings images	• Understand the impact of empathy when communicating and give specific examples of times when they have experienced someone being empathetic towards them whilst making a connection with empathy and a person they can share feelings with.
Reflect on the work covered in the section 'My Behaviour'.	• Complete the worksheet 'time to think'.	workbook, pen, art materials	• Recognise the main learning points from this section of the workbook.

Scheme of work
Section 3 My behaviour

Young person or group _____

Coach _____

Objective	Activity	Resources	Learning Outcome
Understand that behaviour is what we do from simple choices like having sugar in our tea to choosing to deal with conflict with arguments.	• Read the diagrams together and discuss, brainstorm behaviours that the young person does automatically and behaviours the young person chooses.	workbook, pen	• Recognise how others can influence our behavior and begin to explore who may of influenced the young persons behaviour.
Formulate a link between the feelings the young persons experience and the way they behave in response to the feeling.	• Read through the worksheets together and identify what behaviour the young person would display against each feeling.	workbook, pen	• Young person begins to explore and identify a link between certain feelings and their behavioural response.
Select a feeling to explore from the previous task and break down if the behaviour had a positive or negative outcome.	• Write in detail about a situation covered in the work above. Complete the table of positive and negative outcomes.	workbook, pen	• Recognise that behaviour can affect the outcome of any situation in a positive or negative way. • Using a personal experience identify if their own behaviour had a positive or negative outcome and explore alternative behaviors or responses.
Understand the concept of the ABC model, and apply it to personal experiences.	• Read through the ABC sheets together and discuss to ensure understanding, give two examples of situations and the young person is to fill in the 'B' and 'C' section of the table, the young person is then to think of some personal experiences to consolidate learning.	workbook, pen	• Explain how the ABC model works and show understanding that thinking about situations in different ways can affect how you feel about it.
Understand the biological make up of the brain in relation to fight or flight responses.	• Read through 'the brain' together and discuss after each section: the reptilian brain, the limbic system and the neo cortex. • Young person to complete the diagram. • Read 'fight or flight' together and discuss, explore various fight or flight experiences.	workbook, pen	• Recognise how the brain functions and how it can be emotionally hijacked in times when a human feels that its basic needs are being threatened. • Recognise from personal experience times when the young person has had a flight or fight response. →

Objective	Activity	Resources	Learning Outcome
Identify bullying behaviours and different bullying roles.	• Read the section on bullying together and explore the different bullying roles whilst linking the roles to any personal experiences the young person may have had. • List the effects of bullying. • Explore the feeling of power in relation to the bully and the feeling of powerless in relation to the victim. • Research support agencies. • Young person is to produce an individual piece of work in relation to bullying e.g. letter from victim, poster to encourage people to report bullying, newspaper article.	workbook, pen, PC, art materials	• Explain the difference between bullying and non bullying behaviour. • Identify the three categories of bullying. • Identify the effects of bullying. • Understand power in relation to bullying. • Locate various support agencies in relation to bullying. • Present an individual piece of work on the topic of bullying.
Reflect on the work covered in the section 'My Behaviour'.	• Complete the worksheet 'time to think'.	workbook, pen, art materials	• Recognise the main learning points from this section of the workbook.

Scheme of work
Section 4 My relationships

Young person or group ....

Coach ....

Objective	Activity	Resources	Learning Outcome
To identify that some relationships that we have with the people around us can be both positive, negative or both.	• Using the social circle from 'All about me' section write next to each person something about the relationship with that person.	workbook, pen,	• Young person recognises positive and negative aspects of the relationships they have.
To list the important people in the young person's life.	• Complete the worksheet comparing important people five years ago to the important people today. • Choose one important person and research them in depth.	workbook, pen	• Young person can appreciate that over time people that were important to us can sometimes become unimportant. • Young person begins to explore their chosen young person to gain a better understanding as to why they are so important.
To identify an important object from childhood.	• Young person remembers an important object from childhood and fills in the question sheet.	workbook, pen	• Young person can recognise that objects can also have special meaning and evoke various emotions when remembered.
To recognise healthy and unhealthy aspects of different relationships, in particular be able to identify abuse.	• Read through the worksheets and answer the questions – discuss each question and give support where necessary.	workbook, pen	• Young person is able to identify unhealthy aspects of a relationship as well as abuse. • Young person can identify different kinds of support for relationship difficulties.
To recognise the importance of respect in relationship.	• Read through the worksheets together and complete the questions.	workbook, pen	• Young person can identify which feelings are associated with respect, including showing respect, receiving respect.
To recognise that loss comes in many different forms. To identify from personal experience a loss, this could be a person, an object, a pet etc.	• Read through the loss worksheets together, coach to give an example that fits into the loss cycle – young person then to identify from personal experience an example.	workbook, pen	• Young person can use the loss cycle to explain associated feelings. • Young person is able to list many types of loss.
To recognise that remembering special people can have therapeutic benefits and can help to build a sense of belonging.	• Read remembering together and identify a person that the young person wishes to remember – write a letter to the person • Make a collage of all the important people	workbook, pen, art materials, photos, glue	• Young person can identify information that they want their chosen person to know in a letter. • Young person is able to assemble a collage of all the important people in their life to represent a sense of belonging. →

Objective	Activity	Resources	Learning Outcome
To recognise many different types of change.	• Read through changes together and complete the worksheets	workbook, pen	• Young person can begin to recognise many types of changes from physical to unexpected to things they cannot change at all.
To understand Maslow's hierarchy of needs.	• Read through Maslow's theory together and complete the worksheets to ensure understanding	workbook, pen	• Young person can relate Maslow's theory to personal experience and begin to see why basic human needs have to be met.
To recognise that all people experience life-changing 'change'.	• Complete 'it changed my life' questionnaire on young person and two other volunteers.	workbook, pen	• Young person can begin to appreciate that all people are affected by change.
Reflect on the work covered in this section 'my relationships'.	• My relationships – complete the worksheet 'time to think'.	workbook, pen, art materials	• Recognise the main learning points from this section of the workbook.

Scheme of work

Section 5 My self-esteem and confidence

Young person or group _____

Coach _____

Objective	Activity	Resources	Learning Outcome
Understand the meaning of self-esteem.	• Read the worksheets together and check out the young persons understanding with questioning.	workbook, pen	• Explain the meaning of self-esteem and put into own words what is meant by the term.
Explore own level of self-esteem.	• Read through the worksheets together to understand the importance of self-esteem, complete the task exploring their own self-esteem by filling in the diagram.	workbook, pen	• Young person begins to explore and identify a link between self-esteem and where it comes from.
Identify where self-esteem comes from and how it develops over time.	• Complete the 'accepting yourself exercise' and fill in the table.	workbook, pen	• Explain where self-esteem comes form and recognise the things about themselves that they cannot change, talk about why each one of these is important for making them individual.
Explore what has influenced the young person's self-esteem.	• Go back to the table and identify all the things that the young person is not so happy with and begin to explore what has influenced this.	workbook, pen	• Explain how negative self talks etc. influences self-esteem over time.
Understand that taking care of yourself is part of how much you value yourself.	• List all the things that the young person does to take care of themselves.	workbook, pen	• Young person is able to formulate a link between taking care of yourself, valuing yourself and your level of self-esteem.
Explore the power of language.	• Read through the worksheets together and complete the list of positive and negative language, complete the second table and list all the positive and negative words. • The young person from their personal experience is to think of examples of times when they have used both positive and negative language and write about each.	workbook, pen, PC, art materials	• Young person is able to identify examples of positive and negative language and explain the consequences of each.

→

Objective	Activity	Resources	Learning Outcome
Understand that praise can have an impact on self-esteem.	• Read through praise section together and answer each question discussing each one.	workbook, pen	• Young person is able to explain the effect of praise and understand that praise can be difficult to accept if it is something they are not used to.
Understand that compliments can have an effect on self-esteem.	• Read through compliments section together and answer each question discussing each one. • Young person is to decide on a compliment they can give themselves and practise it over the coming week.	workbook, pen	• Young person is able to explain the effect of compliments and understand that compliments can be difficult to accept if they are something they the young person is not used to.
Reflect on the work covered in the section 'My self-esteem and confidence'.	• Complete the worksheet 'time to think'.	workbook, pen, art materials	• Recognise the main learning points from this section of the workbook.

Scheme of work
Summary

Young person or group _____

Coach _____

Objective	Activity	Resources	Learning Outcome
Recap on all the main learning points of each section.	• Read through the worksheets together then look back over each section of the workbook, decide on the main points learnt in each section and fill in the worksheets: – All about ME – My feelings – My behaviour – My relationships – My self-esteem and confidence.	workbook, pen	• Recognise the main learning points and explain how each point of learning has influenced the young person.
Recognise the skills that have been developed over the time spent working on the workbook.	• Read through the worksheets together and tick each skill the young person feels they have developed.	workbook, pen	• The young person is able to identify that a variety of skills have been developing whilst working through the workbook.

General guidance to all facilitators

Throughout this guidance where it refers to 'young person' it assumes that it could be more than one.

Before using the workbook it is recommended that the facilitator reads the entire programme so that they have a thorough understanding of the content. It is likely to take two hours, and this time should be as part of the preparation process. It will also give the facilitator a chance to screen the material so they can remove any parts of the workbook they feel, in their professional opinion, would be inappropriate. For example, the young person may be displaying behaviours that are triggered by specific subjects that the workbook is directing them to explore. In this case the content should be removed or skipped unless the facilitator is a therapist, counsellor or psychologist who has judged that it is appropriate.

After reading the entire programme the facilitator will be informed enough to judge if it is appropriate to use the sections as stand alone sessions or to run the full programme.

It is also essential for the facilitator to have prior background knowledge of the young person and in most cases it would be beneficial to have read their chronology if it is available. This is so the facilitator has an idea of the types of experiences the young person has been through and what parts of the workbook are likely to trigger difficult emotions.

During each session the facilitator must engage the young person in discussion about the material in the workbook and the related creative activities of the topic. Each session is designed to be a time for emotional awareness and personal development, not academic progress. The facilitator must structure each session to recap previous learning and summarise the session as it draws to a close. If the facilitator can see the young person is distressed or finding it difficult to talk about a particular topic, the session should be restructured in such a way that the young person's mood is brought back up towards the end. Otherwise, this could have a detrimental impact on the young person. The workbook should, on the whole, be a positive experience.

When the workbook is run as a full programme, time should be spent on the activities in the section 'all about me' to encourage a positive and trusting relationship. It is possible to add other starter exercises to the current content of the workbook if the facilitator feels it is beneficial in helping build the relationship. This will vary from young person to young person and should be judged on an individual basis according to their responses.

Each young person should have their own copy of the loose-leaf pages bound in an A4 ring binder. Often young people are more willing to buy into something when they feel it is important and worthwhile. It adds quality and kudos to the programme when young people are presented with their own ring binder with quality printed pages rather than photocopies. It also conveys a sense that you are investing in them so they feel the work is important and valuable, often stirring more interest. The loose-leaf page format allows the young person to add additional pages that they create or print out from the internet, and the ring binder protects the material from becoming damaged.

The structure of each session

5-10 minutes	• Greeting and check how the young person is • Recap last session • Collect in any homework set • Offer to do the reading and writing
45-50 minutes	• Engage in the main activities • Discussion work etc. • If the young person is distressed during this work the facilitator must begin to bring their mood back up 20 minutes before the end of the session.
5 minutes	• Recap on the material covered today • Set any homework • Thank young person for participation

Each session should be prepared so that it follows on from where they left off the previous week. The workbook is split into topics with each new topic under a new heading. It may be appropriate, if a topic comes to a close a bit early, for the left over time to be used to play a game. However it is also acceptable for the session to end in the middle of a topic.

Before each session the facilitator should prepare a recap of the previous session to consolidate the learning and give the young person an opportunity to agree with or change the work they produced. At this point the scheme of work can be checked so that the resources can be gathered. The facilitator should then skim read the pages that they expect the young person to cover so they can prepare a homework exercise for the following week if appropriate. If the facilitator is a teacher they can prepare a lesson plan.

It is also important for the facilitator to check with the young person's carers or parents to see if there have been any recent issues that may affect their mood or ability to engage. If there have been significant events that have unsettled them it is better to choose something from the workbook that is less threatening, even if this means skipping forward a few pages. If the facilitator has a positive and trusting relationship with the young person they may be able to ask them if they feel up to working through that particular section. Preparation is the key to a successful session and being informed is an integral part of preparation.

At the end of the session the young person should be thanked for their participation. The workbook should be kept by the facilitator and stored in a safe place to prevent the workbook from going missing or becoming damaged. It is important that the young person trusts their facilitator to keep the workbook safe, as most of them feel very precious about the content and would not like to think that any other young people or staff are reading it, especially those who have been working on a one to one basis. Homework, if there is any, should be given out at the end of the session in preparation for next time. Carers or parents may need to be informed of the homework as some young people will need assistance, encouragement or reminding. The facilitator should give carers or parents any relevant information and then complete any paperwork needed to record the session (lesson plan for teachers, therapy notes for psychologists etc.).

The scheme of work should be used as a planning aid to check whether any special equipment is required for the session, and to allow time to check access to the specified websites on the internet if safety filters are installed. Some internet filters are extremely sensitive and block even the most innocent sites. Even if there are no filters installed it is still useful to check the specified sites to see if there have been any changes to the material or games and that content has not been removed since the time this workbook went to print. It can also be used to help set information-gathering tasks, for example, collecting photographs or other material as homework that will prepare the young person for the following session.

Timing, when being used as part of PSHCE during education

My Personal Development Workbook should take about an hour to run once a week. Young people can arrive at any point in the academic year and the time slot should be scheduled into the timetable as soon as the curriculum manager feels it is appropriate. This works best if it is timetabled as soon as possible as the young person is more likely to accept the workbook if it is seen as a regular part of the school week. In other circumstances it may be decided that a settling in period is required for the young person to familiarise themselves with their new staff and surroundings so that they feel more able to discuss personal issues, and thereby make the workbook more effective. As the pace of the workbook is set entirely by the young person it is difficult to estimate how long the workbook will run for. Experience has shown that on average it has run for approximately one school year when the young person has engaged consistently each week.

Timing, when being used outside education

It is again strongly recommended that *My Personal Development Workbook* is run for an hour a week each week (or by YOT workers every other week). It is important to consider if a settling in period is required when a young person is new to the placement. It is possible for the workbook sessions, even though facilitated by non-teaching staff, to be scheduled into the school timetable of the unit or organisation. This can sometimes assist in encouraging the young people to participate, as education is an accepted part of most young people's day. Often reward schemes are in place for engaging in education, which is another incentive. If there is no education provision available, timing should be judged on the young persons individual needs.

Guidance to all facilitators on the first session

An explanation of the workbook should be given to the young person. This should include an overview of the kind of work that will be undertaken and the expectations the facilitator has about how the young person should participate.

If the workbook is being delivered on the timetable in an education setting the facilitator should introduce themselves as a 'coach' rather than a teacher. This is to clearly make a distinction between workbook sessions and other lessons. This is explained more fully in the guidance for teaching staff. Other professionals can either use the term 'coach' or keep to their usual professional title, although throughout the worksheets the term 'coach' is used when addressing the facilitator.

It should be explained that as the workbook is young person led, if they find anything uncomfortable to write or talk about then it would be skipped until the young person is ready to go back over that particular section.

It is often beneficial for the facilitator to write things down in the workbook as the young person dictates. This gives the young person more time to think, often enabling them to open up and share more thoughts and experiences. Young people who find literacy challenging, will find it a relief to have the facilitator taking on this role. This should always be offered at the start of each session as some young people do enjoy this aspect.

Some organisations have specific paperwork as standard such as confidentiality agreements or teacher student contract's. If any paperwork is to be signed by the young person/ people it should be done during the first session.

When working with a young person who has a history of aggressive or inappropriate behaviour it must be decided where support staff should be if they are required. It may be possible for them to be outside the room but within earshot. It may, or may not, affect the level at which the young person engages if support staff are present but this can be discussed whilst setting the ground rules if appropriate.

Checklist of points to be covered in the first session
- The introduction of the 'coach' if they are a non-therapeutic professional.
- An overview of the workbook – what it is about? How long will it run for?
- What can they expect? What is expected from them?
- The aims of the workbook.
- The option for coach to read from and write in the workbook on behalf of the young person.
- An explanation that the workbook is young person led and that if they feel unable to complete a section it is acceptable to return to it at a later date.
- An explanation of any rewards for engaging in the session.
- An explanation that reports will be compiled about the sessions and the progress the young person is making.
- An explanation that lesson plans, therapy notes or other records will be kept.

- An explanation that homework may be set.
- An explanation of the limits to confidentiality and disclosures.
- To set ground rules. The young person should take part in setting the ground rules as they are more likely to stick to them – even if they have made only a minor contribution.

It is important for the facilitator to be as open and honest as possible whilst discussing and explaining all the bullet points set out above as this will all help forge a positive relationship.

Examples of ground rules may be:

- **1:1 tuition:** being punctual, trying to get through the work set as a follow through programme, no aggressive behaviour, mutual respect.
- **Tuition in groups:** punctuality, listening to others, valuing others opinions, taking turns to speak, respecting others, a group confidentiality agreement – keeping issues discussed within the group.

Guidance to teachers and learning mentors

For teaching staff in residential units, secure and mental health units it is recommended that the workbook should be used as a full programme from start to finish. It can be included in the timetable and delivered as (PSHCE) lessons. As the workbook has many cross-curricular links as well as containing many of the SEAL themes it is a useful tool to include educationally when mainstream resources are inappropriate for looked after young people or other young people with complex needs. The delivery of the workbook can be written into the young persons personal education plan (PEP) and for those young people who have statements of SEN the workbook often addresses statement targets around behaviour, raising self-esteem and appropriate expression of emotion.

It is recommended that the teacher facilitating the workbook does not teach the young person for any other lessons. This is to distinguish what happens in workbook sessions from other lessons that are taught under usual classroom conditions. During the workbook sessions, as already mentioned, it is appropriate for the facilitator to do the reading and writing. This may cause problems if the facilitator then teaches a science lesson and the young person expects the same offer of reading and writing to apply. It may also be confusing for the young person to be encouraged to talk and share information during the workbook sessions but not in other lessons. To avoid all these potential issues the workbook facilitator should only have that role with the young person and should be referred to as the 'coach' rather than 'teacher' so the distinction between workbook session and other lessons is as clear as possible.

It is appropriate that some behaviour that would not be tolerated during usual lessons is allowed to take place in workbook sessions. Young people often find that communicating uncomfortable information is easier when they are hiding their face or fiddling with a pen or doodling. This is a judgment call for each facilitator and is something that could be discussed in the first session when the ground rules are set, if you anticipate this could be a problem.

When the workbook is facilitated by teachers or learning mentors at a therapeutic residential, mental health or secure unit It is recommended that the facilitator forges strong links with the young person's therapist. It is of great benefit to have a weekly handover with the therapist to discuss issues that have been covered and to report on how each session has gone. As some of the material in the workbook has a therapeutic dimension it is important to discuss this crossover so that the work completed in the workbook session complements the therapeutic work.

When using the workbook with looked after young people, young people with statements of SEN and young people who have complex needs who attend a mainstream school or PRU. The workbook should be treated as a full programme and young person taken out of normal lessons to have one to one sessions with their coach in place of PSHCE. Many young people are withdrawn from the classroom for additional literacy and numeracy support so this would not seem unusual.

The curriculum manager and senior leadership at the school may also take this into consideration by providing a more personalised programme for the young person if it is felt that the mainstream curriculum is inappropriate and if the human resources are available. Again, the delivery of the workbook can be written into the young person's PEP and if they have a statement of SEN the workbook can be used to address specific targets.

Guidance to therapists, psychologists and counsellors

The workbook can be used by therapists and psychologists during their sessions with young people in a variety of ways by:

- Following the full programme with the option of adding in therapeutic tools (read guidance on continuity).
- Using it as an engagement tool in the first few months, guiding the young person towards engaging in therapy.
- Using specific sections of the workbook as a base to explore different issues during the sessions.
- Using the workbook as a structured way of engaging them in conversation at the start of each therapy session.

Some young people have great difficulty in engaging with therapy. They may find it difficult to forge trusting relationships with adults, or they may feel there is a stigma attached to therapy therefore, if they engage, this must mean that there is something wrong with them. Some young people are told they must engage in therapy as part of their placement and others struggle to work in the unstructured way that some forms of counselling promote. It is appropriate for therapists, psychologists and counsellors to take specific parts of the workbook in isolation and work through these sections with the young people. This obviously would be done only after working with the young person for some time and building up to working on the specific issues.

Guidance to professionals that work with young people who offend

Professionals who work with young people who offend can use the workbook as either a full programme from start to finish (read 'continuity' guidance) or as a resource from which to select sections to add additional value to programmes that are already in place. The workbook can be used as a bi-weekly tool, as in most cases professionals involved in Youth Justice alternate structured programmes with one week of activity. This is an accepted practice as it has been found that young people at risk of offending respond more positively to 'one week on one week off'. It is important to consider that this way of working will effectively double the predicted length of time the workbook is expected to run, therefore, planning is essential and if time is limited it may be more appropriate to use specific sections of the workbook. It is possible for professionals who work with young people who offend to be highly creative and flexible during the sessions and bring in other specific topics when it is appropriate. For example, work around victim awareness could be covered during the section on exploring values and empathy.

Guidance to social workers, residential social workers and foster carers

Social workers can use the workbook as either a full programme (read 'continuity' guidance) or as a pick 'n' mix toolkit when approaching sensitive areas with a young person. It can be used as an invaluable tool to facilitate relationship building and engagement supplement to the Looked After Children's (LAC) or Integrated Children's Systems (ICS) documentation. The workbook may also be facilitated by staff close to the young person, for example residential social workers or key workers. In these cases the workbook should be run as a full programme adding in additional appropriate material when required, such as material on self-harm.

It is also possible for foster carers to facilitate the workbook although it should be considered that the young person might respond more positively if someone other than a primary carer is the facilitator. The delivery of the workbook can be written as part of the young persons care plan detailing by whom, when and where it will be delivered. The workbook can be a useful programme to work through when the intention is to eventually start life story work: the workbook can even form part of the information gathering towards life story work.

Confidentiality when delivering the workbook

If the workbook is being used in a teaching or non-therapeutic capacity it must be emphasised that personal life experiences and feelings can be discussed on a more private level with appropriate professionals within your organisation or by an identified therapist. Even when this distinction is made, because of the nature of the workbook and the background of looked after children, it is still possible that young people could make disclosures during the sessions either verbally or in written form.

It is essential that the limits to professional confidentiality are covered in the first session, making clear that any disclosures, safeguarding matters or concerns will need to be recorded and passed on to relevant people within your organisation and possibly to the Local Safeguarding Board. Each organisation has their own policy on disclosures, confidentiality and safeguarding so it is essential that you are totally familiar with them and adhere to them at all times.

Risk assessments

In some circumstances it may be important to write a risk assessment around the delivery of the workbook. Risk assessments for individuals may be written to address any particular foreseeable risks and specify actions if things don't go to plan. Group risk assessments may also be written to ensure the safety of the young people within a group, by specifying actions to minimise risk.

When things don't go to plan

It is important to consider that some young people struggle to engage with anything that involves looking at 'self'. When this happens young people often employ distraction techniques. It is important to steer them back to the content of the workbook each time, as they may be testing the boundaries to see how much they can avoid or get away with. Experience suggests that to some degree or another, all young people will refuse to engage in some sessions until they have become used to the content of the workbook and the boundaries that have been set. Consistency is very important and even if they have begun a pattern of persistent refusal it is important to continue to turn up as usual for each session with the assumption that they will engage. Even though this can be frustrating, experience suggests that eventually they will engage once they feel comfortable enough, and familiar with the facilitator.

If the workbook is being delivered to a small group

The needs of groups are slightly different. The following section describes suggestions for implementing the workbook in a small group setting.

There are some limits to working in a group, the main one being that the facilitator is only able to write things down for one young person at a time, and only if the young person feels comfortable enough to allow this to happen. For some young people this will have no adverse affect, but for young people that have been identified as needing extra literacy support, this could hinder the effectiveness of the workbook as often these young people will want to write a minimum amount and can sometimes find it difficult to put their thoughts and feelings into words. The facilitator should offer to do the reading but if one young person would like to read aloud for the group then that would be fine.

The pace of the emotional development workbook is led by the young person so in a group setting the group as a whole will set the pace. This means that some members of the group may be need to work a little quicker and others a little slower. This is something that should be managed by the facilitator and if necessary more or less time should be given for each activity to keep the momentum of the group going.

It is possible that the young people will participate on a more superficial level in a group setting as some young people will view sharing their own personal issues with other young people too much of a risk. It is also possible, at the other end of the scale, for some young people to feel safer working in a group as it can help them feel less isolated when they hear other young people's experiences and hence more confident to share their own. The group facilitator must consider the most appropriate setting for each young person, whether it be better for them one-to-one or in a group.

The young people in the group must be considered carefully as the dynamics will impact on the effectiveness of the participation and learning. If there are strong personalities in the group this must be managed well so that every young person feels that their opinions are valued. The ground rules, confidentiality and boundaries of the group must be explained in the first session as the workbook encourages each young person to discuss their own experiences, which can be very difficult even in the most secure group setting. Given this, the group could be encouraged to work in pairs to start with, as this can help the group form more quickly. They should be encouraged to share their experiences with the group and take turns in feeding back their work. The facilitator must ensure that they give adequate attention to each young person, encouraging interest and involvement.

When a young person moves placement part way through the workbook – continuity

The best interest of young people who are looked after and those with complex needs can sometimes mean that they are moved unexpectedly. This is not ideal in terms of the workbook, but there may be scope for it to be continued at their new placement. Whenever this happens the current placement should always ensure that the workbook is forwarded on with the young person as, even if the workbook is not continued, there is still value in the work already completed. The young person should also have the opportunity to keep and review the work. If the new placement decides to continue the workbook, a facilitator should be identified and time should be given for the young person and facilitator to forge a relationship. Reviewing the completed work together and engaging in the 'getting to know you' activity in the first section could do this. Alternatively, the facilitator could use other relationship building tools for a period of time before returning to the workbook where the young person left off. It is important to ensure that the first session at the new placement covers the check list for the first session and in particular outlines the boundaries and confidentiality, as it would be wrong to assume that they are the same for each organisation.

The effectiveness of the workbook is based around the relationship between the facilitator and the young person. Therefore, when being delivered as a whole programme, it is important wherever possible for the facilitator to commit to delivering the workbook until it is complete.

The end of the workbook

Once the workbook is complete it remains the property of the young person as a piece of work they can reflect on. If the young person is in a residential setting it can be stored by the facilitator or care staff in a safe place allowing the young person access to look back over it whenever they like. When the young person moves placement or leaves care they should take the workbook with them. It is possible, if it has not already been done at a previous placement, to begin or continue life story work once the workbook has been completed. By now the facilitator will have been working with the young person for some considerable time and it is a recommendation of life story work that a relationship is built with the young person for at least six months prior to its commencement. Some of the material completed in the workbook can form part of the life story, such as the family tree, role model work and special things. If the young person completes a collage of important people in the 'my relationships' section, that can be included too. For more information on life story work see Rose and Philpot, 2005.

How to measure the effectiveness of the workbook

During its development the workbook was included in the holistic care package we offered each of our young people. Dr Jane Toner, Clinical Psychologist, used the Strengths and Difficulties Questionnaire (SDQ) (www.sdqinfo.org for further information) to measure the effectiveness of the workbook. We found it to be a useful tool, as it measures the young person's behaviour, emotions and relationships.

The SDQ is a self-report measure that can be completed by the young person, but also by their carers and teachers to gather their perspective as to whether they feel change has taken place. A baseline can be established when starting the workbook and follow up questionnaires easily measure how effective the workbook has been and can highlight specific areas that have improved. The SDQ is easily accessible to most professionals including therapists, social workers and educational staff and is relatively quick and easy to complete, either by hand or on line. (Goodman, 2001; Mathai *et al.*, 2002). It seems to be an appropriate comprehensive common tool and is accepted worldwide for evaluating specific interventions. If it was felt that the SDQ was not appropriate, there are many other tools available on the market that measure emotional literacy which may be just as suitable.

References

DCSF (2005) *Social and Emotional Aspects of Learning (SEAL): Improving Behaviour, Improving Learning*. London: DCSF. http://nationalstrategies.standards.dcsf.gov.uk/primary/publications/banda/seal

Goodman, R. (2001) Psychometric Properties of the Strengths and Difficulties Questionnaire (SDQ). *Journal of the American Academy of Child and Adolescent Psychiatry*, 40, 1337-45.

Mathai, J., Anderson, P. and Bourne, A. (2002) The Strengths and Difficulties Questionnaire (SDQ) as a Screening Measure Prior to Admission to a Child and Adolescent Mental Health Service (CAMHS). *Australian e-Journal for the Advancement of Mental Health*, 1, Issue 3.

Rose, R. and Philpot, T. (2005) *The Child's Own Story. Life Story Work With Traumatised Children*. Jessica Kingsley.

The remainder of this book, pages 1-183, is a reproduction of the workbook for young people, *My Personal Development Workbook*.

For information on how to buy copies of the workbook for work with young people, please see page G10.

Please note that you may not create complete workbooks by copying pages 1-183 from here. But on page G10 you will see that you do have some special and restricted copying permission.

MY PERSONAL DEVELOPMENT WORKBOOK

A step by step workbook for getting to know myself better

My Personal Development Workbook has been created by
Kathryn Plant of Meadows Care (www.meadowscare.co.uk).

For information on how it can be used, please see pages G6-G36.

Introduction

This workbook is made for you to work through at your own pace guided by your coach. The workbook is a programme that helps to develop personal and emotional skills and raise self-awareness. It covers many different topics and includes many different activities: once your file is complete it is yours to keep. The more honestly you work through the workbook the more you will get out of it. There are no right or wrong answers, it is about working through the pages and writing in answers that are personal to you. Your coach is not there to judge your answers; your coach is there to support you while you work through the pages of the workbook. You can use drawings in your work, cut stuff out of magazines or copy song lyrics – anything you feel helps to express yourself!

The websites referred to in this workbook existed at the time of print. Users should check all websites to see if they have changed and substitute other references where appropriate.

Contents

© Kathryn Plant 2011 *Personal Development Matters* www.russellhouse.co.uk

All about ME

All about ME

This is the longest section of the workbook. It is broken down into sections under sub headings and by the time you reach the end you will have explored many aspects of yourself including your image, culture and values. You should know yourself a little better and your coach will have a better understanding of what you are about.

Some of the stuff in the worksheets can be tricky to fill in as the information you will be writing is personal. This may seem really strange at first as it's not something we often do, but the more you do it the more comfortable it will become, and remember, the more honestly you work, the more you will get out of the workbook. Check this out with your coach if you are finding it difficult and they will be able to guide you through.

Your coach will need to check you have internet access to the following websites:

- www.bbc.uk/science/human body
- www.bnfl.org
- www.googleearth.com

Below is a list of resources that you will need for this section:

- stopwatch
- a photograph of yourself
- glue
- scissors
- large roll of paper
- marker pens or felt tips
- tape measure
- computer and internet access
- printer and paper
- balloon
- PVA glue mixed with water (for papier mâché)
- old newspaper
- paint, brushes and pot of water
- bowl
- a photocopy of page 34

"You try finding out why you are you, and not somebody else..."

Ezra Pound

I know I'm out there somewhere

This section is about you finding out about your identity, that means who you are, what you look like, what you are into, what your personality is like, what your values are and what your world is like for you.

So go ahead find out what makes you YOU...

Introductions

Time for you and your coach to get to know each other.

On the next two pages there are two questionnaires with identical questions, one for you to ask your coach and the other for your coach to ask you.

If there is a question that you don't want to answer its OK you don't have to.

Hopefully, by the end of the questions you will know each other a little better.

Getting to know you questionnaire

- What is your name?

- How old are you?

- What is your favourite TV programme?

- What is your favourite food?

- When did you last laugh out loud?

- What is your favourite animal?

- What are your top three films?

- What music are you into?

- Have you ever owned a pet?

- What was the last thing that you drank?

- What is your favourite colour?

Getting to know you questionnaire

- What is your name?

- How old are you?

- What is your favourite TV programme?

- What is your favourite food?

- When did you last laugh out loud?

- What is your favourite animal?

- What are your top three films?

- What music are you into?

- Have you ever owned a pet?

- What was the last thing that you drank?

- What is your favourite colour?

Physical me

Get to know the physical you

```
┌ ─ ─ ─ ─ ─ ─ ─ ─ ─ ─ ─ ─ ─ ─ ─ ─ ─ ┐
│                                   │
│                                   │
│                                   │
│                                   │
│          STICK A PHOTO HERE       │
│                                   │
│                                   │
│                                   │
│                                   │
│                                   │
└ ─ ─ ─ ─ ─ ─ ─ ─ ─ ─ ─ ─ ─ ─ ─ ─ ─ ┘
```

Look at the photo and describe yourself:

What are you wearing?

What are you doing?

Where are you?

How old are you in the photo?

What my body can do

Try each of the tasks below to see how your body works, record the answers next to the questions and get your coach to join in too, you will need a stop watch for some of them...have fun!

How many star jumps can you do in 30 seconds?

Can your tongue touch your nose?

Can you do a press up?

How many times can you tie your shoelaces in 30 seconds?

Can you rub your tummy and pat your head at the same time?

Can you bend your thumb back to touch your wrist?

Can you cross all of your fingers?

How many pin steps can you do in 30 seconds?

How many times can you hop on one leg in 30 seconds?

Can you cross your eyes?

Can you cross your toes?

Can you wiggle your ears?

Can you roll your tongue into a 'U' shape?

Can you click your fingers on both hands?

Can you roll your 'R's?

How long can you stand on one leg without losing your balance?

How many of the above challenges can you combine and do at the same time?

And which ones are they?

What physical challenges did you like?

What physical challenges didn't you like?

What did you learn about your body?

Getting the measure of me

Step 1 – Lie down on the floor on a big bit of paper and let your coach draw round the shape of your body, if you don't fancy having a lie down for 10 minutes there is a body outline on the following page that's already made up.

Step 2 – Take some measurements the length of your leg, the length of your arm, the circumference of your head. Write down the different measurements next to the relevant bit of your body on the outline.

Step 3 – Colour in your outline and fill in the details. Think about the colour of your hair, your skin, your eyes, the shape of your mouth, any freckles, birthmarks, scars and all the little details.

Step 4 – Now draw on clothes and accessories (go wild – use your imagination).

Step 5 – Look again – have you missed anything out, does anything need changing?

Step 6 – Now write your thoughts about what you see...

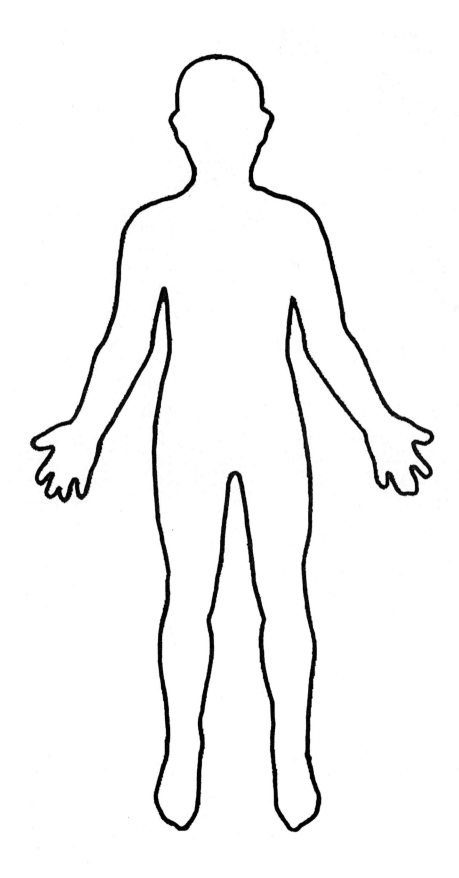

Social me

Our social life can be about our friends or family coming to hang out at our house or the clubs and groups we go to.

It can be about the gang we hang around with or people we do hobbies with, sometimes it's about doing something specific like playing football or dancing and sometimes it's just about standing around spending time with your mates.

Sometimes different social stuff involves different people in your life who may not even know each other.

Our social life is very important because it connects us to the world outside our homes and gives us a greater sense of belonging.

Social life means lots of different things to different people so let's find out what it means to you.

First of all fill in...

My social life questionnaire

1) What do you do socially?
   - Go out with friends.
   - Go to a club or activity.
   - Stay at home.
   - Go to school or college.
   - Or something else (write it here).

2) Who is part of your social circle?
   - School friends
   - Family
   - Friends from home
   - Staff
   - Or other people (write them here)

3) What social settings do you feel comfortable in?
   - Parties
   - Activity clubs
   - Family activities
   - Home
   - Anywhere else (write here)

4) Who do you feel most comfortable with?
   - Large groups of people
   - Small groups of people
   - Family
   - Friends
   - Anyone else (write here)

So what have you found out about your social life? Write your thoughts about it here…

My social circle

Our social circle is about the people we spend our time with, the people we hang out with, the people we go to clubs or groups with and the people we meet up with to do stuff like going to the cinema.

The people in our social circle can be mates, family, staff, youth workers or people we only see at a certain group or club.

They can be male or female, any culture, any race or any age and they are really important to helping us feel we belong.

In our social circle we could have people who are really close but might not be family, or maybe best friends who we might see once a week or less.

Our social circle is about placing people we have relationships with in a position that represents how important they are to you.

Now, think about your social circle and complete the one on the following page, put the people you know into each circle starting with the ones closest and most important to you in the circle nearest to ME and working your way out.

Remember you can have as many people as you like in each circle.

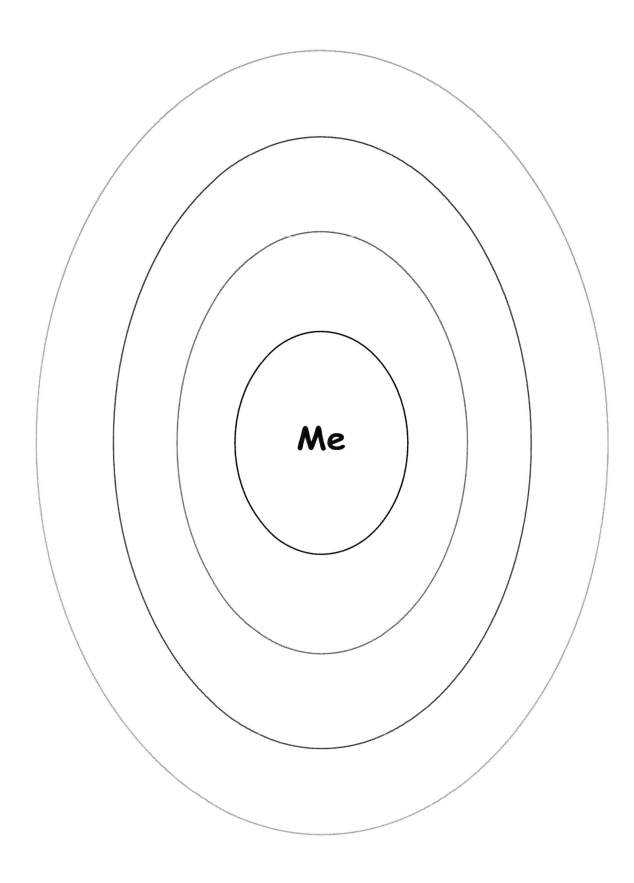

My social environments

Now let's think about your social environments, where do you go, where do you hang out, who with?

Think of as many as you can and write or draw them here, also think about the distances you have to travel and pop that in too.

Now choose three of the social settings describe them in more detail:
- What do they look like?
- What do you do there?
- How do you feel there?

Setting 1

Setting 2

Setting 3

My social life

Our social life can depend on what's happening to us and where we are.

Think about your social life a year ago...how has it changed and what does each gain or loss means to you?

Change	Gain	Loss

Summing up my social life

Use this page to list your social activities and your social people starting with your favourite and working your way down.

My culture

Our culture can help us to feel we belong, can give us an identity and can influence what we eat, how we interact, what we believe in. It can be about the colour of our skin, the religion we practise, the music we listen to, the activities we attend. For some people their culture is a very important part of how they see themselves, for others rejecting their cultural heritage helps them to be individual and for many it simply doesn't matter. What does your culture mean to you and how important is it?

Let's find out...

Cultural identity

This bit is about looking at some of the important areas that help us to identify with a specific culture.

Start by circling all the words that apply to you in each of the boxes.

If we've forgotten something please add it in.

Ethnicity

This is the colour of your skin, your racial background and the part of the world you come from, you can include other members of your family if you feel they are part of your ethnicity.

Black	Irish	Japanese	White	Asian
	British	African	Middle Eastern	
Scottish		Mixed Race	Chinese	European
	Western	Caribbean	East European	

Religion

This is about a religion that you may have been brought up in or that you practise now.

Hindu	Atheist	Jehovah's Witness
Catholic	Muslim	Buddhist
Jewish	Protestant	Agnostic
Orthodox	Janian	Christian

Language

There are approximately 270 different languages spoken in Britain, which languages do you speak?

English	Urdu	Cantonese	Polish	Latvian
Korean	Arabic	Spanish	Gaelic	Sign
French	Welsh	Punjabi	Hebrew	Gujarat
Mandarin	Japanese	Russian	German	

Traditions

These are ideas, customs, beliefs and activities that are passed down through generations and are important in shaping a culture. Traditions can be specific to a country, a city, a village, a religion or even a family. Examples of traditions are Sunday dinner, haggis, the village fete, getting married at a young age, and supporting a specific football team. Think about some of the traditions in your culture and record them below:

Food

Festivals

Dance

Clothes

Music

Anything we forgot?

Role models

These are people past and present who we copy and try to be like because we admire their beliefs and values. Each culture has their role models e.g. Jesus, Martin Luther King, Buddha or even your local religious person or teacher. It can also be someone from youth culture like a singer or actor, or even someone from your family.

Try writing a list of all the people you can think of who are, or have been role models to you throughout your life.

Decide on two people who you see as cultural role models. Do some research on them and create an A4 sheet each to say who they are, stick in photos, write some information and include why they are your role models. Once it's complete pop it into your file behind this page.

Culture and gender

Sometimes different cultures have different ideas and expectations about each gender. Sometimes these views can be very stereotypical. For example there may be an expectation that as a female you will grow up and stay at home to look after children, or as a male you will follow tradition and work in the industry that your father worked.

What does your culture say about your gender?

How do you feel about this? Do you agree or disagree?

Culture and sexuality

Some cultures have very specific ideas and viewpoints about sexuality. These are usually very strong beliefs along with sometimes evidence from different religions.

What does your culture say about sexuality?

How do you feel about this? Do you agree or disagree?

Other cultures

When we don't understand other peoples cultures prejudice can occur. Prejudice is when you unfairly and unreasonably dislike something or someone without enough thought or knowledge, this often has a harmful or negative effect.

Think of an example of prejudice, this could be something you have experienced or maybe something you have seen on the television or in a film. Write about it below…

Talk about the example with your coach and discuss how you feel about prejudice. Write your thoughts about it here…

The effects of prejudice can be terrible. Sometimes it can be ignorance or a lack of knowledge that creates prejudice. If you have people around you, especially ones that you admire, who are prejudiced, it can be difficult to disagree with their values and sometimes it's just easier to go along with what they think. The diagram below is an example of how we can overcome prejudice. We should always strive to be moving towards the right.

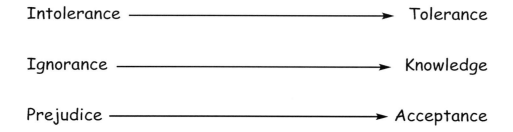

Intolerance ——————————→ Tolerance

Ignorance ——————————→ Knowledge

Prejudice ——————————→ Acceptance

Sonia Bellamy, Hyde Clarendon College, 2008

Time to think

Now is your chance to think a bit more about the work you have just done about your social life and culture.

Here are a few questions to get you going:

- What three things have surprised you most?

- What did you already know?

- What three things are you most proud of?

- Is there anything you would like to do more of or change?

Use this page creatively to express your social life and culture.

Write a poem, draw, doodle – whatever you like.

My image

Our image is what we show to other people by what we wear, how we speak, the music we listen to, the activities we do, the people we hang out with...it may not be who we are inside, but it can be who we want other people to see us as.

Like belonging to a cultural group, our image can help us feel we belong to a social group. Unlike a cultural group, which is one we are born into, we can choose our image and we can change it when we want.

Some of us have a definite image that we like to be part of; some of us borrow lots of different bits from other groups, some of us don't identify with any image in particular and for some of us it's not important.

Your image is your personal choice so let's find out what image means to you...

What is image?

Image means different things to different people, some groups of people have a certain image they like to show, particularly some groups of young people. Do some research and tell us what the different groups below are about. Print some images from the internet; remember to look at clothes, music and activities because it's all part of what makes up the image. Once you have printed stuff out stick them onto A4 paper, if you're feeling really creative do an A4 sheet for each group.

Here are some groups to get you started

Goths	Emos	Chavs	Hoodies
Indies	Moshers	Others?	

Which groups do you like?

Why?

Which groups do you not like?

Why?

Which group do you feel part of, if you don't feel part of any if you had to choose which one would it be?

Why?

What is MY image?

Let's get personal, look back at what you have done so far...

What does your photo and body drawing say about your image?

What do your friends, favourite things and places tell you about your image?

What does your culture say about your image?

Can you give your image a name? Do you belong to a particular group? if not can you invent one? Write or draw about it here...

Clothes

Music

Dance

Activity

Words

Finish this sentence:
My image is...

My values

Our values are about the things we believe in, feel strongly about and give us our own individual rules to live by. If we know what our values are and can stick to them, then we can be true to ourselves in the way we live our lives. Let's begin to explore your values by doing our questionnaire.

What's important to YOU questionnaire?

Read the following statements and using red (very important) yellow (quite important) and green (not very important) felt tip pens, put a dot next to each statement reflecting how important each is to you. There is no right or wrong answer this is about how you feel.

- How other people see me is important.

- I want people to trust me.

- I try hard to achieve what I set out to do.

- I make sure that I look after myself because I'm worth it.

- I believe things should be fair for everyone.

- I think we should look after people who are more vulnerable.

- Sticking to rules is really important.

- I believe in speaking out when I think something is wrong.

- I enjoy having money and possessions.

- I think I should work hard for what I want.

- I feel strongly about helping others.

- I admit when I am wrong.

- I believe that it is important to look good and be fashionable.

- People should fight for whatever they believe in.

- I think that everyone should have the freedom to do what they want.

Now write down your top five important statements here and add a sentence saying why these things are important to you:

1

2

3

4

5

My values table

Make a copy of this page, then from that copy cut out and read the statements, discuss them with your coach and decide if you think they are OK or Not OK or you're just Not Bothered. Then stick them in the column of your choice on the page after.

Your mate's girlfriend is being really rude to him – he slaps her and calls her a cheeky cow.	The government proposes National Service to stop gang culture and yob violence in Britain.
Your friend confides in you that her boyfriend is pressuring her into having sex and is saying he will dump her if she doesn't. Your friend doesn't want to lose him so plans to sleep with him even though she is not sure if she wants to.	You are out on the street with friends and some of them start to verbally abuse a stranger because they don't speak English and are wearing clothes of their culture.
The school leaving age is being raised to 18.	You see two boys kissing and holding hands in a shopping centre.
There are 12 major species of animals including pandas, tigers and orang-utans facing extinction in our lifetime due to losing their natural habitat and illegal poaching.	You have been grounded for a month because you have come home very late three nights in a row and you have seemed spaced out.
You see someone dropping a glass bottle in a park and walking away.	You see a woman verbally abusing a police officer because she was stopped for speeding in a school zone.

My values table

It's OK	Not bothered	It's not OK

Dilemmas

Sometimes in life it can be difficult to make a decision because the best choice for you might not agree with your beliefs.

For example – you are out with a group of friends and one of them gets really drunk and throws a brick through a shop window. The others run away and leave you with your mate who threw the brick; you can hear the Police sirens getting closer. You have to decide whether you are going to stay with your mate or run too because you are already in trouble with the Police and don't want to get accused of damaging property.

Think about it, talk it over with your coach, what do you think you would do?

Look at the following dilemmas and see where you stand, is it ever okay to:
- Tell on someone
- Lie about something
- Use violence
- Break the law
- Force somebody to do something
- Ask somebody to lie about something

What decisions were easy to make? Do you know why that was?

What decisions were hard to make? Again do you know why?

Now, talk to your coach about a dilemma you have had and how you dealt with it, write about it here.

Who do you look up to?

Our beliefs and values can come from anywhere, we can be influenced by TV, books, magazines and music but most often we get our values from the people around us.

OK, choose someone that you look up to, this can be someone in your life or a film star, singer, celebrity etc. and answer the questions below.

- Who is it?

- What is it about them that you admire?

- What do you think their values are?

Now do the same thing for someone that you **don't** look up to.

- Who is it?

- What is it about them that you don't admire?

- What do you think their values are?

My life rules

Time to look over the work you've done in this section and decide what your values and beliefs are. Write yourself a set of rules that you want to live your life by that will help you to stay true to yourself.

Raising self-awareness

'Know thyself'

Plato Ancient Greek Philosopher 427BC

Raising your self-awareness helps you to know and understand yourself better. Try these simple exercises and see how far you can raise your awareness.

Place yourself on the 'Ladder of Self Awareness'

Top of the ladder
I totally know myself!

Bottom of the ladder
I don't know myself at all!

Now write down five likes and five dislikes (this can be anything – food, music, people, TV)

Likes

1)

2)

3)

4)

5)

Dislikes

1)

2)

3)

4)

5)

Let's look at your favourite things to do.

Write a list, do a drawing, make a collage, go ahead this page is yours:

Have a think about the things you are good at and the things you feel you could be better at. This time think of stuff you do and the kind of person you are.

Name three practical things you are good at.

Name three things about your personality that you like.

Name three achievements and say how you feel about them.

Now for the stuff that you feel you could do better:

Name three practical things that you could improve if you tried.

Name three things about your personality that you'd like to work on.

Name three things that you wish you had done differently and how you feel about them.

Next step, thinking about situations and feelings, finish these statements:

- I love it when…

- I don't like it when…

- I feel happy when…

- I feel upset when…

- I feel angry when…

- I feel confused when…

- I feel excited when…

- I feel scared when…

Positive qualities

Look at the list below and circle or highlight the positive qualities you feel you possess. Add your own words at the bottom if we have missed any.

accepting	energetic	mature
accurate	enthusiastic	modest
adventurous	fair	neat
affectionate	flexible	optimistic
ambitious	forgiving	organised
artistic	friendly	original
bold	funny	patient
calm	generous	peaceful
careful	gentle	polite
caring	good-natured	pleasant
cautious	happy	punctual
cheerful	healthy	quiet
compassionate	helpful	realistic
confident	honest	reliable
considerate	hopeful	resourceful
cooperative	imaginative	responsible
courageous	independent	sensible
creative	intelligent	strong
curious	inventive	talented
dependable	kind	trustworthy
determined	light-hearted	trusting
eager	likeable	understanding
easy-going	lovable	unique
efficient	loving	witty

Looking at all the positive qualities that you highlighted, what are your ten strongest positive qualities?

1

2

3

4

5

6

7

8

9

10

Let's take another look at the 'Ladder of Self Awareness'

Top of the ladder
I totally know myself!

Bottom of the ladder
I don't know myself at all!

Has anything changed in how well you know yourself?

Time to think

Now is your chance to think a bit more about the work you have just done on your values and self-awareness.

Here are a few questions to get you going:

- What three things have surprised you most?

- What did you already know?

- What three things are you most proud of believing in?

- Is there anything you would like to do more of or change?

Use this page creatively to express your values and self-awareness

Write a poem, draw, doodle – whatever you like.

My personality

Now we've thought about self-awareness let's move on to looking at your personality. This is the biggest part of what makes you **YOU**. It's about your behaviour, your temperament, your feelings, and your thoughts that all add up together to make the whole, individual you.

First of all, visit these web sites and try the personality tests and see what they say about you...Have fun! www.bbc.uk/science/human body. Try the:

Necker Cube Experiment
Face Perception Quiz
Perfectionism Quiz
Personality Quiz

What did the tests get right or wrong?

What did you learn about your personality?

Three things you already knew:

Three things you didn't know:

Now try a multiple intelligence test and find out in what ways you are smart. www.bgfl.org

Print out the diagram and put it in your file behind this page.

OK, let's see who the real expert is on you. Do this quiz yourself and ask someone else to do it about you as well (this can be family, staff, friends whoever you feel could give good answers).

On a scale of 1 to 10 where do you think you fit

	1	2	3	4	5	6	7	8	9	10	

tidy   messy

introvert   extrovert

passive   bossy

approachable   unapproachable

trusting   suspicious

follow the rules   rebel

thoughtful   thoughtless

serious   joker

selfless   selfish

gentle   tough

nervous   confident

lethargic   energetic

optimistic   pessimistic

reserved   friendly

Now look at your answers and your partner's answers, carefully.

What are the similarities?

What are the differences?

Do you agree with any differences?

Any surprises?

My personality wall

Imagine that our personalities are like walls, they have solid foundations that keep the wall strong and then lots of different bricks cemented together to build the wall up. The foundations are the bits of our character that are the biggest and strongest and are always part of us no matter what. Then there are the different size bricks that we add on to make our personalities full. Talk to your coach about the different bits of your personality and look back at the work you have just done, decide on which parts are your foundation and then build your personality wall from there.

My personality wall

Time to think

Now is your chance to think a bit more about the work you have just done on your personality.

Here are a few questions to get you going:

- What three things have surprised you most?

- What did you already know?

- What three things are you most proud of?

- Is there anything you would like to do more of or change?

Use this page creatively to express your personality

Write a poem, draw, doodle – whatever you like.

Use this page creatively to express your personality

My place in the world

Understanding where we fit in geographically and socially with our families helps us to have a sense of belonging and a place in the world.

Time to get messy!
You may want to protect your clothing as PVA glue once dry won't wash off clothes or surfaces so clean it up straight away.

Make a globe with your coach out of papier mâché. This can be done by covering a balloon with ripped up pieces of old newspaper covered in PVA glue diluted with a little water. The more layers you give it the stronger the papier mâché will be, once you have covered it enough tie string around the knot and hang it up to dry.

Now, access googleearth.com try putting your address in and see what comes up.

Zoom in and out and see if you can recognise roads or buildings in your area. Now look at places you used to live, old schools, relatives or friends houses, places you hang out or used to hang out etc.

Print out the images and add them to your file behind this page, write on them what the places are and what they mean to you.

Time to get messy again!

Get the papier mâché globe that you made, pop the balloon and decorate it with paint to represent the globe. It doesn't have to be perfect just roughly recognisable. Once you have finished you can balance it in a bowl and leave it to dry again.

British Isles connections

Now let's have a look at your British connections. Fill in the British Isles map on the next page and mark down all the connections you have, think about home, family, friends, school and clubs etc.

Now look at your map and answer these questions:

- Do you have lots of connections in the same area?

- Are they spread out over the country? Or are they in clusters around the country?

- How far do your connections spread (if you don't know how many miles it is you can take a guess)?

Go back to your globe.

Have a look back over your culture and image etc. and mark on your globe in felt tip where these influences have come from. You could do this by writing on white stickers so you can see what is written more clearly or if you're feeling really creative stick the stickers on cocktail sticks and stick them into the globe.

Think about the kind of music you like, the food you enjoy, family or friends that live in a different country, places where you have been on holiday or would like to visit.

For instance if your favourite food is Pizza then put a mark on Italy.

If you're into Beyonce's music put a mark in America.

Family tree

Now you have a sense of where you are geographically let's see how you fit within the people in your life. This family tree can include whoever is important to you not just blood relatives, so think about all the important people in your life and complete the tree on the next page.

Now looking at your family tree, record your thoughts and feelings about where you fit...

Time to think

Now is your chance to think a bit more about the work you have just done on your place in the world.

Here are a few questions to get you going:

- What three things have surprised you most?

- What did you already know?

- What three things are you most proud of?

- Is there anything you would like to do more of or change?

Use this page creatively to express your place in the world

Write a poem, draw, doodle – whatever you like.

My feelings

My feelings

In this section you will learn about feelings. This may sound quite simple but feelings are quite complex to understand. All feelings are OK but it's the way you choose to express those feelings that can sometimes determine whether you end up in trouble, jeopardise relationships or never get your point across. You will learn how to identify your own feelings and begin to recognise what is happening in your body physically when you experience some emotions.

You will also begin to look at some of the trickier feelings and become equipped with strategies to help control some unhelpful ones.

This section also explores the effects of sharing feelings with someone you trust and suggests ways to communicate more effectively with the people around us.

Below is a list of resources you will need for this section

- feelings images
- computer and printer
- A4 paper
- felt tips or craft material
- a photocopy of page 68

My feelings

When stuff happens we have feelings. Our feelings can make our bodies react in certain ways and can make us think and behave in certain ways. The way we feel helps us understand what is going on for ourselves and what is going on for other people. Understanding our own feelings means we can get on better with others, say what we need and want, and behave in a positive way.

So let's find out about feelings...

What are feelings?

In the dictionary it says that:

Feelings are emotions that manifest and have a physical effect on the body.

Have a look in the dictionary or on Wikipedia and see what other meanings you can find, print them or write them out and put them in your file below.

Basically, feelings are something we all get all the time. They are something that we physically feel in our body and sometimes it is difficult to know where the feelings have come from or why we feel them at all. Sometimes we can get lots of feelings all at the same time and sometimes you might think that you feel nothing.

Sometimes feelings can seem to come out of nowhere and sometimes feelings can be so overwhelming that it can be difficult to know what to do or how to react. Often the hardest thing is to share your feelings with someone, but before you can share them you have to figure out what feeling it is that you have and that's not always so easy.

So to get started...think about all the feelings you have on a day-to-day basis and answer the following:

When my alarm goes off or when someone tells me it's time to get up I feel...

When I am in my least favourite lesson I feel...

When I am watching my favourite TV programme I feel...

When I am listening to my music I feel...

When it is time for bed I feel...

Now let's try playing feelings bingo...have fun!

Make a copy of page 68, then from that copy cut out the feelings bingo cards, give them out and ensure that everyone has a pen.

One person needs to be the bingo caller. The bingo caller acts out the list of feelings below one by one.

The players shout out guessing what the feeling is that the bingo caller is acting out.

Once the correct answer has been shouted, all the people with the correct answer on their bingo card crosses it off. Keep going until one person has crossed off all the feelings on their card: they shout out bingo and they have won.

List of feelings for the bingo caller to act out....

Bored	**Angry**
Sad	**Shocked**
Scared	**Smug**
Shy	**Confused**
Surprised	**Disgusted**

Bored	Angry	Smug
Sad	Shocked	Shy

Shy	Disgusted	Angry
Confused	Sad	Scared

Angry	Smug	Disgusted
Surprised	Scared	Shocked

Confused	Shy	Bored
Sad	Disgusted	Shocked

Non-verbal communication

We first know how somebody else is feeling through their facial expression and body language. In fact studies have shown that 93% of communication is picked up non-verbally and only 7% by the words actually spoken.

So, being able to recognise the feelings of other people is a social skill that will help you make friends and fit in, it will also help you to make decisions about what actions you might take.

Having the ability to read emotions is a skill that helps people to enjoy and succeed at life.

Have a look at the photos on the next few pages and write on them what you think the person or people are feeling.

Your own non-verbal communication

How you sit, stand and hold your arms, your posture and the expression on your face gives other people clues about what you are feeling and the sort of mood you are in. Sometimes if you are unaware of your own body language you could be giving off the wrong message without even realising.

Other people remember body language and it is reported that it is the most remembered element when forming an impression. Having good posture, standing tall and being relaxed all helps with looking and feeling confident.

Eye contact is important to looking and feeling confident too. When you don't have eye contact, if for instance you look down, it may communicate that you feel rejected and looking elsewhere than the person you are talking to may communicate that you are bored. Holding good eye contact (remember not to stare) will suggest that you are confident and are communicating openly.

All of the above are tips on how you can begin to control your body language. It can also help you to read other peoples body language too.

Adjectives for feelings

You might have noticed that there are lots of different words for expressing the same feeling, which can get really confusing. Play the feelings word game and see which column you think each feeling belongs.

cheerful	miserable	hostile	uneasy
delighted	discontented	joyful	scared
irritated	petrified	anguished	glad
resentful	worried	furious	overwhelmed
elated	down	blissful	pleased
terrified	satisfied	anxious	outraged
threatened	mad	excited	distressed
devastated	frightened	hurt	frustrated
aggressive	ecstatic	enraged	panicky
stressed	despairing	nervous	bothered
annoyed	upset	apprehensive	disturbed

SAD	HAPPY	ANGRY	AFRAID

Okay, time to get personal, get to know you own feelings by rating your emotional profile. Tick the correct box for the frequency you feel each emotion.

Emotion	Never	Sometimes	Often
Happy			
Angry			
Lonely			
Loved			
Helpless			
Hateful			
Excited			
Calm			
Bored			
Worried			
Scared			
Upset			
Belonging			
Sad			
Powerful			
Confident			

Is there anything you would like to change about your emotional profile?

Explore a feeling

Now decide on a feeling that you are going to explore and write it here:

On the body outline on the next page draw and write:

- How the person's body might feel.

- How the person's face might look.

- What kind of thoughts the person might be having and or what they might be saying to themselves.

- What the person might do and how they might sound and behave to other people.

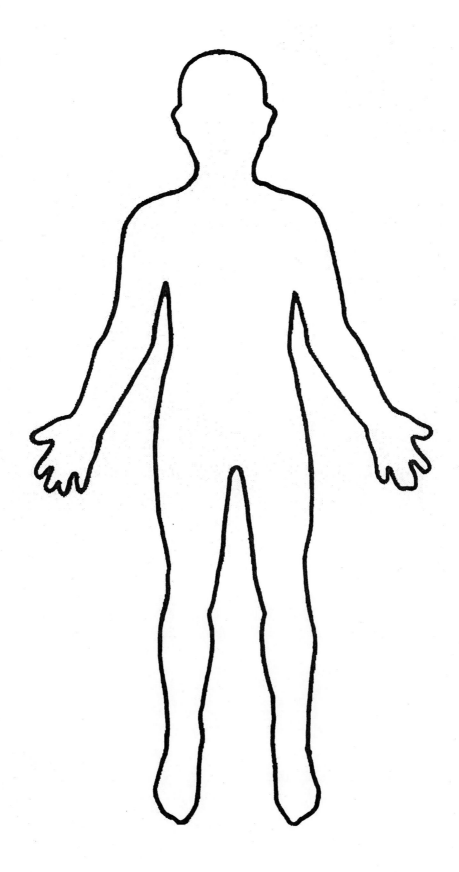

Feeling confident

Feeling confident can be something that doesn't come easy for some people. Sometimes you can feel confident in one area but not in another, and some people just seem to be naturally confident all the time. Being confident can help us to learn and be successful because it's not so scary to try something new if you can bounce back when you get it wrong.

Can you remember a time when you felt confident? Where were you? What were you doing? How did you know that you were feeling confident? Try to be specific, what were your thoughts? What were you feeling physically? Talk to your coach about it and then write about it below. (If you don't want to talk and write about your own experience use somebody else's.)

Feeling confident...

If you are not naturally confident then there are things that you can do to increase your confidence. Set yourself a task that you know you can succeed at, like decorating your bedroom or baking a cake. Even if it doesn't go exactly to plan focus on what was a success and what went right. If you examine the track record of everyone who is successful you will probably find that they failed more times than they succeeded, they just never stopped believing in themselves. Concentrate on the times when you have accomplished what you set out to do and this will help to give you a lasting feeling of confidence.

Tricky feelings

All feelings are OK, but sometimes you need to have feelings that you don't like because they serve an important purpose. Sometimes feelings cause problems, so it is helpful to be more aware of them. That way you might have a bit more control of them when you need to.

For example:
Feeling nervous can be useful, it can be a warning that there is a potentially dangerous situation and you need to be extra careful.

But, feeling nervous can also be a problem. It can prevent you from performing at your best during a sports event, in a test or during an important meeting. If you find that this happens it can help to take deep breaths and imagine you are in a place that you find safe and calm, perhaps your bedroom or on a sunny beach. Imagining yourself being successful or achieving what you are nervous about can help you to feel more confident and your nerves will begin to reduce. Another way of feeling less nervous is by holding or wearing something that we feel gives us luck or helps us succeed, think of footballers who wear their lucky socks or business people who wear their lucky suit or lucky piece of jewellery. It's something that psychologically gives us a little bit of confidence.

Is there something you can think of that would make you feel less nervous and more confident in a stressful situation?

How would you feel if...

We feel different emotions in various situations and often we feel more than just the one emotion. Think about the following scenarios, have a discussion with your coach and record what you think you would feel.

1) As you have been walking through town shopping you slip on a piece of litter and almost fall over.

2) Your computer has just been corrupted by a virus, all your music files have been lost and there is no way of getting them back.

3) You have worked hard on an essay for your favourite teacher; it's taken you several days and was very difficult to do. The teacher starts to criticise your handwriting and seems to be ignoring the work you have done and the effort you have put in.

4) It's your birthday and all the people who you care about are going out with you for a big meal to celebrate.

Sharing feelings

Sharing your feelings with other people can be a daunting thing to do. Some people feel shy about sharing feelings and others might feel like they are risking being judged.

It is good to share your feelings with someone who is a good listener, someone who will not give you advice but listen to what you have got to say and try to understand how you feel. It's easier to share your feelings with somebody who you trust. Once you know who you can talk to, sharing your feelings can help you feel better and can help you to feel closer to the person you are sharing them with.

Sometimes just saying how you feel out loud can help you to feel better. If things are going round and round in your head it can sometimes make things worse and you can become overwhelmed. Having people who you can share your feelings with can be one of the most helpful things in life. It prevents us from bottling everything up. Imagine that you are an empty bottle and every tricky feeling we have is a measure of fizzy cola. Every time you experience a tricky feeling the cola gets poured into the bottle, if you talk about your feelings then the bottle is being emptied. If you don't, then the bottle gets fuller and fuller until it fizzes over because it can't take any more.

Can you think of the people that you feel comfortable sharing your feelings with?

How do you communicate your emotions?

Now, time to look at how you communicate YOUR emotions. Think about the tone you use when you talk, the volume, the speed, your body language and facial expression, record what you would sound like and your non-verbal communication when you are:

Angry

Happy

Excited

Scared

Sad

When did someone listen to you? (Not just hear you)

Still thinking about communication, listening is very different from hearing. Listening requires concentration and for the listener to check out with the person talking that their understanding is correct.

Listening is about keeping your judgements to yourself and not giving out advice or instruction. When you really listen to someone, it gives the impression that you care about them because you are willing to invest the time to just sit and listen. Have you ever heard the phrase 'I have got a lot of time for that person' in other words I value that person so much that I am willing to give lots of my time to them.

Sometimes it can feel like there is not enough time to really listen to people because there always seems to be so much going on and so much to do.

Sometimes, depending on your personality, it can be tempting to interrupt what the other person is saying and talk about your own experience.

Think of a time when somebody really listened to you. What did they do that made you feel listened to and how did it feel to be listened to?

Now think of a time when you didn't feel listened to. What did the person do that made you feel not listened to and how did that feel?

Tips on how to be a good listener

Read the list below and add on any of your own tips. If you know anyone that would benefit from reading the list, photocopy it and hand it to them. If you think that you could improve your listening skills then consciously practise the tips when communicating over the next week and report back to your coach the difference it made.

- Don't butt in when the other person is talking.

- Don't give advice.

- Don't make judgements.

- Don't start talking about your own experiences.

- Don't criticise, or tell them it's not that bad.

- Try to accept how they feel even if it seems like they are over-reacting.

- If it is a problem, don't try to solve it for them, they need to learn from their own experience. If your idea does not work they will learn that you are not to be trusted.

- Nod your head to show that you understand.

- If you don't understand clearly, check it out with them, they will appreciate that you want to know.

Empathy

Empathy is being able to understand other peoples thoughts and feelings and supporting and valuing them. Sometimes the phrase 'being able to put yourself in another person's shoes' is used to describe empathy. It's the ability to show understanding and acceptance and can bring you a sense of emotional connection to the person you are being empathetic towards.

When we understand and respect other people's beliefs, values and feelings we can be more effective in making relationships, working together and learning from people with diverse backgrounds.

Think back to the question that you answered about someone listening to you, and decide if the person who really listened to you was being empathetic? If so what were they doing to show empathy? Record your thoughts here.

Showing empathy when you communicate

When people are communicating they can show empathy in their non-verbal communication. You can show that you are listening by keeping good eye contact and show that you are interested by facing the person you are with.

If you put yourself in their shoes as they tell their story, it will help you get a better understanding and your facial expression will reflect how you feel. If they are talking about a happy time, they may be smiling as they speak. You can share their enjoyment and empathise by smiling along with them. You may already do this, therefore you are already able to empathise!! Can you remember a time when you empathised with someone?

Empathy campaign

Now we are going to plan an advertising campaign encouraging people to use more empathy. Make a poster using the computer, felt-tip, paint or any other craft material and think of a slogan to use in your campaign. It could be something like...

> *'Try to understand somebody's way of seeing things and they will try to understand yours'.*

Or

> *'Walk in the other persons shoes before judging them'.*

Use your imagination and go wild.

Time to think

Now is your chance to think a bit more about the work you have just done about your feelings.

Here are a few questions to get you going:

- What three things have surprised you most?

- What did you already know?

- What three things are you most proud of?

- Is there anything you would like to do more of or change?

Use this page creatively to express your feelings!

Write a poem, draw, doodle – whatever you like.

My behaviour

My behaviour

This section is closely related to the section 'my feelings'. Rather than exploring feelings you will be exploring where your behaviour comes from and how your thinking can influence your behaviour.

You will learn about the fight or flight responses that your brain is programmed to have and will investigate some of your own behaviour that has perhaps been unhelpful.

During this section you will also cover anti-bullying, this can sometimes be uncomfortable especially if you have first hand experience of bullying, so don't forget to talk to your coach.

Prepare to put your thinking cap on, as this section requires a bit of concentration.

Below is a list of resources that you will need for this section:

- computer with PowerPoint or
- A4 paper and craft equipment

My behaviour

Behaviour is shown in the way we act and react in different situations. Some of our behaviour is learnt from the people around us, as well as from the media and books. Some of our behaviour comes from trying to fit in with our peer and cultural groups and some of our behaviour is a reflection of how we feel. Some behaviour is acceptable to us and our society, and other behaviour is seen as unacceptable.

Where does behaviour come from?

It could be something as simple as do you have sugar in your tea?

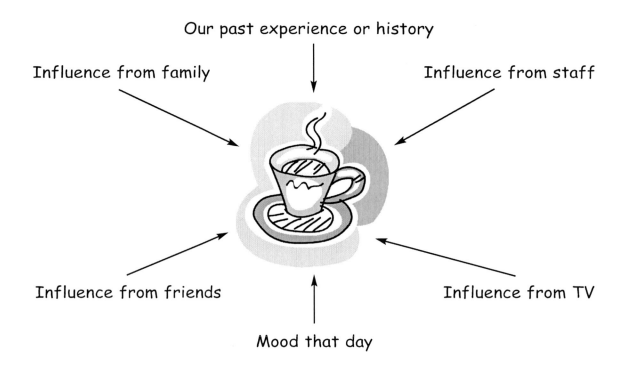

Our past experience or history

Influence from family

Influence from staff

Influence from friends

Mood that day

Influence from TV

Or, do you deal with some conflict by having an argument?

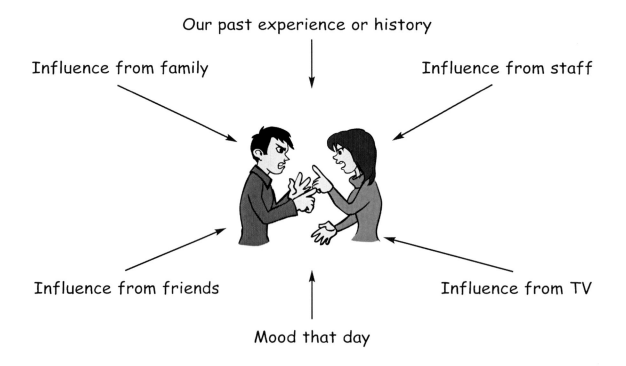

Our past experience or history

Influence from family

Influence from staff

Influence from friends

Mood that day

Influence from TV

Some behaviours feel like we do them automatically because we have learnt them so well and some behaviours we can choose a bit more easily.

Can you think of any behaviours that you do automatically? (drink a certain drink, brush your teeth, bite your nails, any habits)

Can you think of any behaviours that you choose to do? (smoking, drinking, swearing)

Now, think about times when you have experienced the feelings below. Write about how you behave and what you do.

When I feel angry I...

When I feel sad I...

When I feel like people are not listening to me I feel...

When I feel happy I...

When I feel like I can't do something I...

When I feel frustrated I...

When I feel gutted I...

Choose one of the feelings you have experienced from the previous page, go over the situation again and write a bit more detail below...

- Did your behaviour get what you wanted?
- What were the positive or negative outcomes?

Positive	Negative

The ABC model

The ABC model is something that can be used to demonstrate that there a variety of different ways to think about any situation and each results in a different outcome.

Different situations happen every day, the way you think about the situations determines how you feel about it and what you do. Look at the example on the next page and discuss it with your coach. In column A the same situation is happening, column B has different options about how a person might think or feel about it, and column C has different options about what a person might do about it or how they might react.

A What is going on?	B How do you feel and think about it?	C What do you do?
You are walking down the street and your friend passes you, you say 'hello' but she doesn't reply and keeps walking.	Upset and angry that she is ignoring me.	Possibly confront her?
	Upset and angry that she is ignoring me.	Possibly stop talking to her because she has obviously fallen out with me.
	Not bothered, she just didn't hear me.	Possibly nothing, will text her to see if she is OK.

Think about the consequences of each of the behaviours, are they negative or positive? Write next to each consequence a 'N' or 'P'.

Which of the answers above do you think is closer to your thinking and behaviour?

Think of your own examples or if you prefer your coach could give you some typical examples to fill in the tables below.

A What is going on?	B How do you feel and think about it?	C What do you do?

A What is going on?	B How do you feel and think about it?	C What do you do?

Look back at the tables you have just completed. Decide on the thoughts and behaviours that YOU would have for each situation and discuss them with your coach.

Do you notice anything about the thoughts and behaviours you would have?

Are your thoughts positive or negative?

What consequences would your thoughts and behaviours have?

Are the consequences positive or negative?

Emotion and the brain

(This section is based on the work in the secondary SEAL resources.)

To understand our emotions and behaviour better it can be useful to know how our brains work.

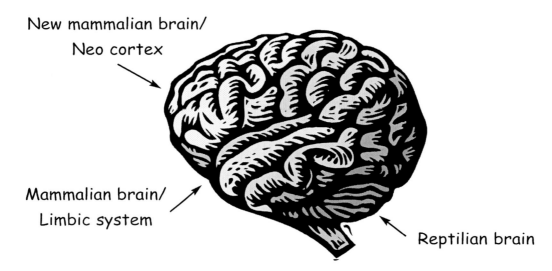

New mammalian brain/
Neo cortex

Mammalian brain/
Limbic system

Reptilian brain

Our brain acts as if it were made up of three different parts. Scientists believe that each of the three different parts was formed at different times of our evolutionary past, from being fish to monkeys and finally humans.

The reptilian brain

The oldest part of our brain is the reptilian brain, it's the part that we share with lizards. This part of the brain works automatically without you knowing it. It controls things like breathing and digestion but it is also the primitive survival part of the brain. Automatic reactions include how we react to save our lives if we are surprised or frightened. If you have ever heard a loud or unusual noise and jumped, that was an automatic response by your reptilian brain. Sometimes people can hit out before they really understand what is going on, again this is an automatic response by the reptilian brain. This type of immediate and automatic reaction is often called 'fight or flight'.

The mammalian brain (the limbic system)

We share the limbic system with mammals. This part of the brain is newer than the reptilian brain and is a lot more sophisticated and sensitive. The limbic system lets all information in through the senses, the information then passes through a little structure called the thalamus. The thalamus sorts the information and then sends it to other parts of the brain to work on. The limbic system is mostly concerned with emotions and feelings and is responsible for what our bodies do when we have strong emotions and feelings. Part of the limbic system is the amygdala which responds very quickly and alerts the reptilian brain to danger or threat.

The new mammalian brain (neo cortex)

This is the newest part of our brain and has only been around for a few million years. Some animals like chimpanzees have this part too, but in humans this is the largest part of the brain. This is the clever or 'thinking' part that can sort out information, use language, do sums, understand science and make sense of the world. It is able to think logically and as far as we know can do all the things that most mammals can't.

So, how does this all normally work?

Information that we see or hear does not go straight to the clever part of the brain (neo cortex) it goes straight to part of the limbic system called the thalamus. The thalamus sort of screens the information to ensure its safe and non-threatening and then sends the information to the clever part of the brain (neo cortex) so that it can make sense of it and work out what to do. Sometimes information might be neutral like 'this is a thing called a door, I need to open it then walk through it'. But sometimes the information might be something to get emotional about, like looking at puppies or getting a nice letter. The thalamus then sends that information to the correct part of the brain and we respond by expressing the way we feel by smiling etc. This is what happens when life is peaceful and there are no threats or unsafe situations detected by the thalamus.

Emotional hijack

So, what happens when the thalamus detects a threat?

If the thalamus believes that the information passing through it is unsafe it reacts differently. Instead of sending the information to the thinking part of the brain it sends it straight to the amygdala in 1/1000th of a second. (Wow that's quick). The amygdala sends signals straight to the reptilian brain to make us react, often by jumping, running away or fighting back. This is the 'fight or flight' response. The body is flooded with stress chemicals and it is a very basic instinctive response; it causes an immediate strong feeling which we usually interpret as fear or anger. We react like this before we are even conscious of it.

This is sometimes called an emotional hijack because the clever part of the brain (neo cortex) is shut down and the oldest part of our brain takes over. This is an automatic protection mechanism that was very useful to our ancestors who needed to escape from dangerous animals. When a poisonous snake or hungry bear is about to attack us we will only survive if we run away first and ask questions later, if we had to think about it first we would be dead.

Label the diagram on the next page to see if you can remember which part of the brain does what. Read this section again if you want to jog your memory – this is complex stuff.

Diagram of how the brain works

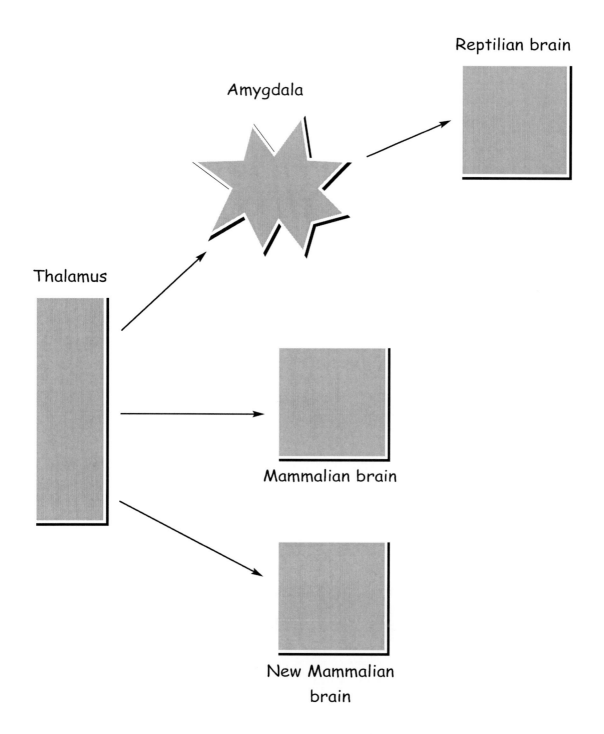

Label the arrows:

Threat detected

Emotional stuff detected

Thinking stuff detected

Living with our brains in today's world

Even though life is very different for us now our brains still work in the same way, we respond to threats with 'fight or flight'. The threats that the thalamus detects are mostly not life threatening, they are often what other people say or do, like your friend saying 'I hate you' or someone pushing you into a doorway. Sometimes the threats are things that go wrong in our lives, usually when we are already upset or on edge, this is when our minds and bodies are already set for feeling threatened or in danger.

So, to put all that information into context, when we are upset or under stress we lose the use of the clever thinking part of our brain. (Have you ever been in a bad argument?) We can't think straight, we might feel confused, might withdraw, runaway, or say and do inappropriate, hurtful, harmful or even violent things. So while it's good to have quick reaction times for speeding cars, falling branches or dangerous situations, sometimes the reptilian brain can hinder our lives, it can break friendships, prevent us from succeeding at school or even get us into a fight.

Fight or flight

Fight or flight responses are very common, they are something that everybody has experienced. Think of a time when your thalamus detected a threat and your reptilian brain responded? e.g. burning your hand or stepping off the pavement in front of a car, hearing a balloon pop unexpectedly. Or maybe you have experienced falling out with someone and you did or said something without thinking about it. Talk to your coach and write about it here.

Look back at the ABC stuff and see if you can identify any fight or flight responses.

Bullying

Most people have been in contact with bullying, whether they have experienced bullying, know or have known someone who is being bullied, or may be using bullying behaviours themselves. It is important for everyone to understand the impact that bullying has and to be able to identify bullying behaviour.

Bullying is deliberately hurtful behaviour that happens again and again with one or more people often bullying the same person.

Bullying is about power and the purpose of bullying is to make someone feel more powerful or to make someone else feel less powerful.

Think for a few minutes then answer these questions:

- What does it feel like to be powerful?

- Can you think of a time when you felt powerful?

- What does it feel like to be powerless?

- Can you think of a time when you felt powerless?

Discuss this with your coach and decide what you think this means. Write your thoughts about it here...

Types of bullying

(Based on work in the *Young Person's Guide to Bullying* by the Children's Safety Education Foundation.)

There are three main categories of bullying:

Physical abuse

This is when a bully uses violence to attack someone by kicking, hitting, pushing or punching. This can even be 'accidental' like tripping someone up or even spitting at them. Bullies can also steal belongings or break or ruin your stuff.

Verbal abuse

This is when a bully uses words to hurt or frighten someone. There are many ways a bully can use verbal abuse they can name call, taunt, threaten, mimic or make you look silly.

Silent bullying

This happens when the bully doesn't say anything at all but they ignore you all the time or try to stop you from joining in. They might send awful notes about you, send nasty text messages, spread rumours or even follow you around to intimidate you.

Is it bullying?

Read the following sentences, talk about it then decide if you think it is bullying, write next to each if you think it bullying or not.

- Leah keeps telling Lauren to wear deodorant.

- Amy has got eczema and some girls in her class say that she has got lizard skin, always avoid her and talk behind her back.

- Jake spits into a can of cola and says he will make Kieran drink it.

- Finlay accuses Raja of stealing his game and they have a fight at break.

- Kade has got a lisp and some people in his class try to make him say words that he struggles with.

- Anna and Grace won't let Emma play with them.

- Every time Bailey walks into the room a group of young people start to giggle and whisper.

- Adam has a disability which means that he cannot always control his movements. When he gets excited his hands jerk up. A group of boys mimic him whenever he tries to join in the football game.

- Steven and his friends threaten Callum every playtime, this time they took his dinner money.

- Jamie and Joshua grabbed Jack's bag, tipped everything out and kicked his stuff all around the floor.

For all the situations that were just incidents rather than bullying, what do you think would turn it into bullying?

Some effects of bullying

Bullying can be very serious, the person who is being bullied can be left feeling terrible, it can seriously affect their self-confidence and self-esteem. In the most severe cases they can even begin to hate their life and learn to stop trusting people. The effects can last a long time even if the bullying has stopped, they can find it difficult to make friends and can feel lonely and isolated.

Anyone can bully another person. It could be an adult that bullies a child, a younger child bullying an older or taller child, a child bullying a child of the same age, an adult bullying another adult. Bullies come in all shapes and sizes and so do victims, but the effects of bullying are similar.

Try to add to the list below some more effects of bullying:

- Loss of self-confidence
- Not eating
- Uncontrollable crying
- Headaches
- Not being able to sleep
- Feeling afraid
- Not wanting to go to school
- Having nightmares
- Becoming quiet
- Becoming moody
- Stomach aches
- Becoming nervous
- Feeling lonely
- Running away from home

Bullying roles

The ringleader (bully) Initiates and leads the bullying but not always the person doing the bullying.

The victim (target) The person who is being bullied.

Assistants Are actively involved in 'doing' the bullying.

Reinforcers Support the bullying, they might laugh or encourage other people to 'collude' with what's going on.

Defenders Stand up for someone who is being bullied. They know that bullying is wrong and feel confident enough to do something about it. This might involve talking to an adult in school or another adult they can trust.

Outsiders Ignore the bullying and don't want to get involved.

Have you been in any of these roles?
Think about a time that you have been in any of the bullying roles...if you have experienced any,

- What was it like?
- How did you feel?
- What did you do?
- How do you feel about it now?

Record your thoughts here. If you have never experienced any of the roles use your empathy and try to imagine what it would be like.

Support

If you are experiencing bullying there are organisations that can help support you.

Child line   0800 1111

www.childline.org.uk

www.nspcc.org.uk

www.beatbullying.org

Now comes the fun bit...

As bullying is so unacceptable it's time for you to get creative with bullying in mind. You can either, design a poster, do a Powerpoint presentation, write a poem or a letter. You can make it from the bully's point of view, from the victim's point of view or just to get the message across that bullying is 'Not OK'.

Time to think

Now is your chance to think a bit more about the work you have just done about your behaviour.

Here are a few questions to get you going:

- What three things have surprised you most?

- What did you already know?

- What three things are you most proud of?

- Is there anything you would like to do more of or change?

Use this page creatively to express your behaviour!

Write a poem, draw, doodle – whatever you like.

My relationships

My relationships

In this section you will explore the relationships you have with all the different people in your life. You will look at characteristics that make relationships healthy or unhealthy and explore how respect affects relationships.

During this section you will also cover the loss cycle which can be applied to relationships you have lost or that you feel you have lost. You will be covering work on changes that have taken place and learning how different people respond to change. This section also looks at remembering people and things from your childhood that were special to you.

You will also look at Abraham Maslow's hierarchy of needs, gain an understanding of his theory and apply it to your own life situation.

Some of the work in this section is quite deep so let your coach know if you are finding it tricky and they will support you trough the content.

Below is a list of the resources that you will need in this section:

- photos of the important people in your life
- glue
- scissors
- piece of A3 size card

My relationships

We have relationships with the people who are around us such as family, friends, carers and other significant people.

Some people we have great relationships with and others not so great. Some relationships can be healthy and some unhealthy.

Sometimes you have to have relationships with professionals like teachers, social workers, managers or key workers.

Relationships can be tricky and are not always easy to maintain.

Whilst some relationships might feel like they have been taken from us others can make us feel important and cared for.

You may like some relationships and dislike others.

Social circle again!

If you completed the 'All about me' section, look back to the 'Social me' page where you completed your social circle. Take the page out and decide if you would like to update or change it. There is a blank social circle on the next page if you want to use it instead.

If you have not completed a social circle before, complete the one on the following page, putting on it all the people who you have a relationship with. The people who you feel closest to should be placed nearest to 'ME' in the centre.

Your social circle might include those with whom you have negative relationships as well as those that you are more positive about. You can show this by where you place them in the circle, or you could go over your social circle and write next to each person, in a different coloured pen, something about the relationship you have. (This might be if you feel it's a positive relationship or if you like the relationship etc.)

If you have used your social circle from 'All about me', once you have completed the task above photocopy the updated social circle and pop it into your file behind this page.

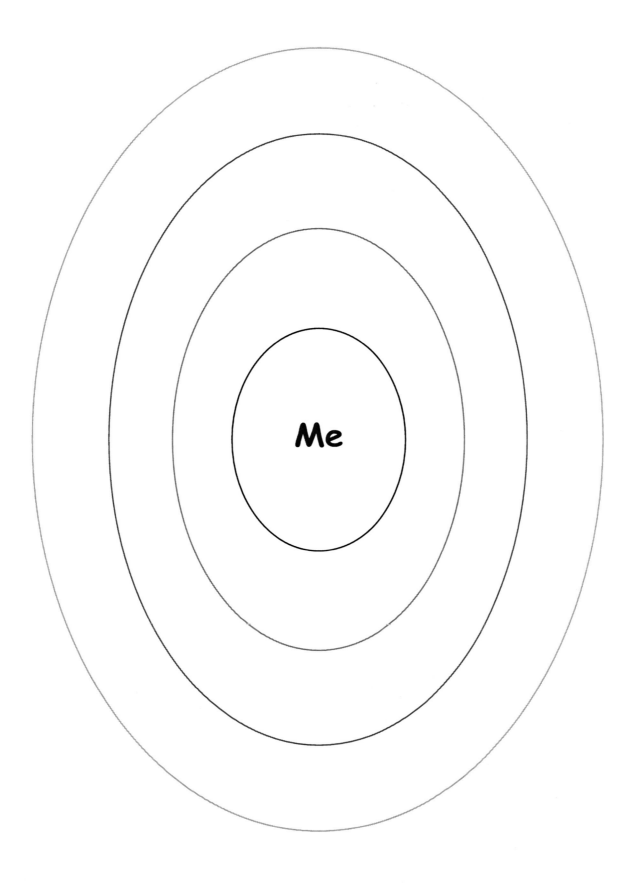

As time goes by people who were important to you five years ago may no longer be important, or there may be new people in your life who might be important to you now. Complete the table below: some people might belong in both columns.

Important people in my life five years ago	Important people in my life now

Choose five people from your list and talk to your coach about how you met, when you last saw them and what is special about them, record your thoughts below...

1.

2.

3.

4.

5.

Important person

Looking at your list, choose one important person and complete the sentences below about them.

The name of my important person is

My important person likes

My important person has

My important person is sad when

My important person laughs when

My important person is cross when

My important person is special because

Still thinking about your important person, remind yourself of a special time that you shared, where were you? What were you doing? How old were you? How did you feel? Why was it a special time?

Write about it here, you could also try drawing a picture or sticking something in to remind you about it, like some grass or sweet wrappers or anything else that could represent your special time. (Use a separate sheet of paper if you need to.)

Special things

Most of us have special things too. Think back to when you were younger, do you remember having a special thing? It could have been a dummy, a blanket, a teddy or anything else that was special to you.

What was it?

What was special about it?

How did you feel when you had your special thing?

What happened to your special thing?

Draw a picture of your special thing in the box below.

Think about a special thing that you have today, it can be anything that is special to you like a photograph, a teddy, a present that somebody gave you, a piece of jewellery, something from when you were younger it can be anything at all.

What is it?

What is special about it?

How do you feel when you look at your special thing or hold or wear it?

Is there anything else that you can include about your special thing?

Do you have a photo of your special thing? If you do, stick it in behind this page.

Relationships are tricky!

As you grow older and think about getting a boyfriend or girlfriend it's important for you to be able to identify what makes healthy and unhealthy relationships. Relationships change over time and it is important to realise that this is perfectly acceptable.

It is also important in a relationship that you accept the other person as they are and they accept you, if you want to change things about your partner then this is not a good foundation for a relationship.

It's also important to maintain other relationships or friendships so you feel connected to other people not just to your partner.

Indicators that a relationship might be in trouble could be poor communication, unresolved conflicts or insufficient amount of quality time together.

Look at the table on the next page and add some features of your own...

Healthy and unhealthy aspects of a relationship

Healthy aspects of a relationship	Unhealthy aspects of a relationship
Both people accept each other as they are.	Too dependent on the other person.
Both people recognise and appreciate change.	Jealousy.
Each person establishes personal limits.	One person being controlling.
	Both or one person being selfish.
There is a balance between time spent together and apart.	One person not allowing the other person to spend time with their friends.
Both people have separate hobbies and interests as well as mutual ones.	

Being able to identify abuse

Sometimes it may be difficult to admit that behaviours that are abusive are going on within a relationship. Relationships change slowly and we are not necessarily aware of unhealthy aspects creeping in until they are already happening. In the list below are some behaviours that are unacceptable, talk to your coach and see if you can add to the list.

- Being afraid of making the other person angry.
- Being hit or hitting someone.
- Needing permission to do things without the other person.
- Being called unkind words or calling someone unkind words.
- Being afraid that the other person will hurt you.
- Shouting at the other person to get your own way.
- Putting pressure on the other person to do sexual things.
- Being afraid to end your relationship.
- Keeping secrets.

Ending a relationship can be a very difficult thing to do and can sometimes take a lot of courage. It's important to get support from other people so you can talk to them honestly about your feelings, to discuss issues and clarify them. There are also other agencies you can contact for support if you find yourself in a difficult relationship.

www.childline.org.uk
www.getconnected.org.uk

Respect

Part of having the courage to end unhealthy relationships is about respecting yourself, and that is all tied up in your self-esteem. Basically, the more you value yourself the more likely you are to identify and end an abusive relationship.

Think of ways to show respect to other people

Think of ways to gain respect from other people

Who do you respect?
Identify someone who you respect, it could be someone from your family, a friend, a carer or anyone else you know.

Who do you respect?

Why do you respect them?

How do you feel when you know that someone is respecting you?

How do you feel when you know that someone is not respecting you?

How do you feel when you show respect to someone else?

Showing respect

Showing respect is really important to help build good relationships. It can make you feel valued and enables you to appreciate people from diverse cultures and backgrounds. It can help you to enjoy and celebrate difference and diversity and prevents prejudice and discrimination.

Consider whether you can respect everyone.

Talk to your coach and think about the possible barriers to this, write your thoughts about it here...

Loss

All of us at some point or another will experience loss whether it is a toy that you have lost, a PE kit or a pet dying. Sometimes it can feel like you experience losses that other people don't seem to. It could be the loss of a close friend because you have moved area. You have probably already experienced loss even though you might not have thought of it that way. Look at all the examples below and try to add some of your own ideas....

Different types of loss

- Parents getting divorced or splitting up.
- Grandparent dying.
- Losing a favourite possession.
- Leaving your country.
- Having an injury that scars your face.
- Falling out with your friend.
- Changing school.

Discuss with you coach any of the above that you think you have lost.

Understanding loss

When you experience significant loss it can really help to talk to someone you trust about it as this might stop you from feeling overwhelmed.

It might also help to understand the loss cycle. The loss cycle consists of different phases that people are thought to go through when suffering a loss. These can be seen as a progression from one phase to another but there are also times when a person can slip back to an earlier stage or even get stuck in one. There is no right or normal way to experience loss, there is no timescale and each person's reactions are highly individual and therefore the experience will be different for each person.

The process of loss

Disbelief – shock, denial

Recognising the loss – yearning, anger, guilt, sadness, despair, pain

Realisation – sadness, hopelessness, depression, fantasy 'if only'

Acceptance – to move on or re-engage

You can apply the loss cycle to any experience of loss, think about losing a purse or wallet.

Loss of wallet

Disbelief – You look in your pocket and find that it is not there. You check again because you know you put it there. You check your other pockets because you can't believe that it is gone.

Recognising the loss – you begin to feel sad and upset that your wallet is gone along with your money! You feel angry with yourself that you have been so clumsy to lose it.

Realisation – you say to yourself...if only I had been more careful I knew I should have put it in my bag, it would have been safe there.

Acceptance – you go out and buy another wallet and think to yourself that you will be more careful with this one.

Think of another example and explain it to your coach. It may be something like losing a precious item or it may be a person. Choose something that you feel comfortable discussing and write about it below?

How do you feel about it now?

Sonia Bellamy, Hyde Clarendon College, 2008

Remembering

Most of us know somebody that we haven't seen for ages but would like to see. Can you think of anybody like that? It may be a family member, an old friend, a carer or anyone else you can think of.

Talk about it with your coach and write a letter to them, what would you want them to know?

You could tell them what you have been doing, where you are or what it is you miss about them.

Once you have written it pop it in your file behind this page.

Now for fun!

Think about all the important people in your life now and maybe important people in your life that you have never met like a great uncle or granddad and maybe important people who have died. Think of all the things that remind you of these people and collect photographs, things or pictures of things and make a display or collage. Your coach will help you to put it all together and find a brilliant place to put it on display.

Changes

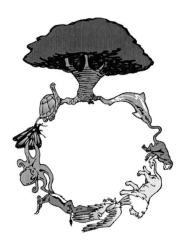

Things around us change all the time, just like we change too. Our bodies change physically, our appearance changes, we might have to start wearing glasses or choose to dye our hair. We could decide to join a club or begin a new hobby. Think back to when you were a baby and write down below some things that have changed about you (it could be your hair colour, you learned to ride a bike, you grew taller, you might live with different people etc.)

What would you change?
Sometimes it can be fun to imagine what it would be like to make changes, what would you change if...

You were the teacher for the day?

You were a social worker?

You were education minister?

Unexpected change

Sometimes unexpected changes can happen that can be difficult to cope with. It might be that you moved house unexpectedly or that you lose contact with a particular person. When unexpected or unwelcome changes happen you may experience a range of uncomfortable emotions and may also experience a sense of loss similar to the work you have just covered. People respond differently to changes and we all have our own history which influences the way we think, feel and behave about change. Humans are programmed to be wary of change because it can threaten our basic needs, similar to the fight or flight work if you completed the section 'my behaviour'. Some people seem to take changes in their stride and others can feel very unsettled and apprehensive about what the change will bring or what it will mean.

Maslow's theory

Abraham Maslow was an American Psychologist and is considered one of the founders of humanistic psychology. In 1943 he wrote a paper that set out a diagram of five fundamental human needs (see below). It is accepted that you start by fulfilling the needs at the bottom of the triangle before moving your way up. The triangle is referred to as Maslow's hierarchy of needs and it is quoted and taught so widely that many people perceive this model as the definitive set of needs.

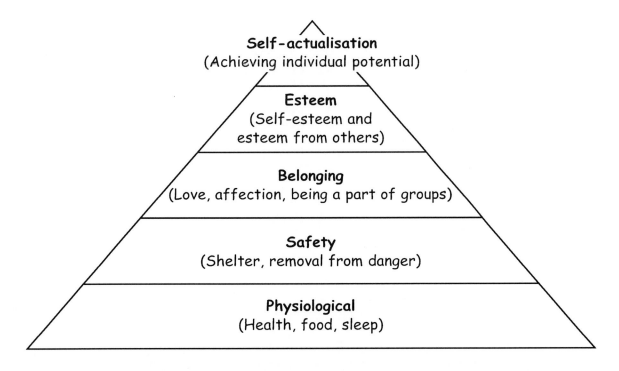

Self-actualisation
(Achieving individual potential)

Esteem
(Self-esteem and esteem from others)

Belonging
(Love, affection, being a part of groups)

Safety
(Shelter, removal from danger)

Physiological
(Health, food, sleep)

What do you think each means?

Level 1 physiological needs

Level 2 safety needs

Level 3 belonging needs

Level 4 esteem needs

Level 5 self-actualisation needs

What does each need mean?

Physiological needs are to do with the maintenance of the human body. Breathing, food, water, sleep and access to a toilet are all basic needs of the human body.

Safety needs are about putting a roof over our heads and keeping us from harm, ensuring that we are in a safe family environment and are protected from illness.

Belonging needs are feeling part of a family or group. Having friends and knowing that we are loved and we love others.

Esteem needs are achieved when we have a healthy level of self-esteem and confidence and feel respected by other people.

Self-actualisation needs are to become the best that you could be, to the maximum ability you have.

How do we meet those needs?

If all your physiological, safety and belonging needs are being met then you will be able to move up the triangle, begin to fulfill the esteem needs and eventually assuming you continue to fulfill the needs, get right up to self-actualisation.

Anything that threatens our ability to meet the needs towards the bottom of the triangle causes us to have uncomfortable feelings to the point of thinking about it constantly. Remember a time when you have been really, really hungry, you can't stop thinking about food or think about anything else properly until you have eaten. Or if there has been trouble in your family, it's difficult to concentrate on anything else until the issue is resolved. These uncomfortable feelings are nature's way of letting us know to be careful in situations that threaten our basic needs. Imagine people living in some third world countries. Even though those people may have loving families and shelter they struggle to get constant access to food and water, this means that their basic needs are never met because there is always the threat of starvation and in worse case scenarios, death.

Everyone has experienced their basic needs being threatened at some point but some people more than others experience events or situations more frequently that can make it difficult to move up the triangle.

Try filling out Maslow's triangle on the next page with information about yourself. Draw the sections on the triangle then include all the needs in each that you feel are being met. Once you have finished talk to your coach about your triangle and record your thoughts about it on the following page.

My thoughts about my triangle

145

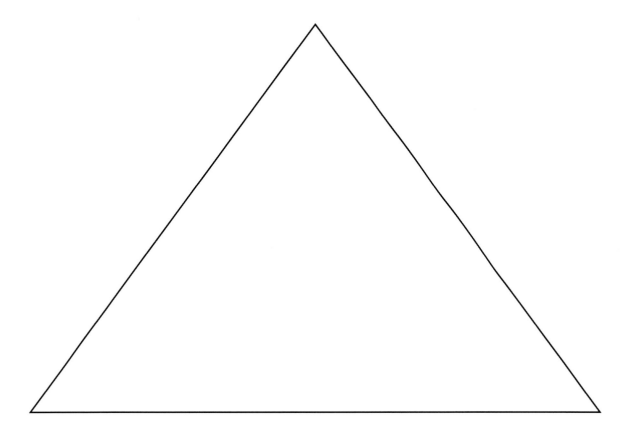

Looking at changes again!

We have looked at the physical changes that take place over time and have looked at responding to changes with apprehension or looking forward to what is in store. But what about the changes that are so big that they change our lives completely. Everyone has experienced some major changes that stick in their memory as being the most significant. Often these events are the ones that evoke the strongest feelings usually feelings of either extreme elation or deep sadness. Complete the questions on the next page then ask two other people to answer the questions too.

It changed my life interview

What was the biggest change in your life?

Did you have any control over the change?

How did you feel before this happened?

How long did it take you to get used to the change?

How did you cope with the change?

Did anything unexpected happen?

If you had your life again would you keep the change?

It changed my life interview

What was the biggest change in your life?

Did you have any control over the change?

How did you feel before this happened?

How long did it take you to get used to the change?

How did you cope with the change?

Did anything unexpected happen?

If you had your life again would you keep the change?

It changed my life interview

What was the biggest change in your life?

Did you have any control over the change?

How did you feel before this happened?

How long did it take you to get used to the change?

How did you cope with the change?

Did anything unexpected happen?

If you had your life again would you keep the change?

It changed my life interview

If you had a magic wand and could change something, what would it be?

You might like to write about something you could change for yourself, or for your family, maybe for your community or even the whole world.

Time to think

Now is your chance to think a bit more about the work you have just done about your relationships.

Here are a few questions to get you going:

- What three things have surprised you most?

- What did you already know?

- What three things are you most proud of?

- Is there anything you would like to do more of or change?

Use this page creatively to express your relationships

Write a poem, draw, doodle – whatever you like.

My self-esteem and confidence

My self-esteem and confidence

In this section you will learn where self-esteem comes from and why it is important. You will begin to recognise your own level of self-esteem and begin to explore ways to increase it.

You will gain an understanding of how being optimistic can help you and how setting goals and destinations can increase your determination and give you a focus.

Explore the power of language and practise praising and complimenting to equip you with the tools to start increasing your confidence levels and raising your self-esteem.

There are some homework tasks in this section so be prepared to practise what you learn and bring back your findings to your next sessions.

The only resources you will need in this section are a pen and two different coloured highlighters.

My self-esteem and confidence

You can't touch it, see it or hear it but your self-esteem is there every day. It affects how you feel, it is there when you look in the mirror and is present every time you talk about yourself.

What is meant by self-esteem?

Below is a list of definitions that can help you gain a good understanding:

- the way you see yourself
- recognising your personal strengths
- accepting who you are
- recognising your own needs
- living by your own values
- respecting yourself
- eliminating negative 'self-talk'
- encouraging positive 'self-talk'
- recognising that you are a worthy person
- understanding yourself

Self-esteem is not:

- how others see you
- how many friends you have
- bragging about yourself
- how clever you are
- how others describe you

Where does self-esteem come from?

 The people around you help to build your self-esteem right from the moment you are born. Positive words and actions help you feel important and good about yourself and encourage you to see yourself in a positive light.

If you are not encouraged enough or if there is shouting and arguing where you live or if you have been bullied or called names it can all contribute to you having low self-esteem. If you have experienced mostly negative feedback from the people around you then it is likely that you have developed a negative image of yourself. It's important to remember that if this is the case it is possible to improve or build upon your self-esteem if you decide that you want to.

Why is self-esteem important?

Healthy self-esteem is important because it allows you to like who you are - warts and all. It's not a short-term feeling, but a deep down strong feeling that you are 'OK'. That feeling gives you the courage to try new things even with the risk that you might not be good at it or even fail. Self-esteem is also what allows you to make healthy choices  and will give you the courage to say no or walk away if your friends are doing something dangerous or something that goes against your own values. You will know that you are worth caring for and will be proactive about looking after yourself.

What is YOUR level of self-esteem?

 Your self-esteem and how happy you are with it need's to be determined by YOU. It's easy in today's society for young people to create an image of themselves based on what they perceive is acceptable and what other people tell them. The media creates lots of pressure for young people to look like the stick-thin tall models with flawless skin with not a spot in sight! What the media doesn't tell you is that most of the images you see in magazines and advertisements have been airbrushed to perfection. Even the people on TV, both male and female are covered in heavy makeup. In reality we all have little imperfections, we are all a different shape, have different skin types, have birth marks, scars, stretch marks, lumps, bumps you name it we all have them, it's what helps to make us unique.

Your self-image is something which has been built up over time and is the mental picture you have of yourself. It is created from personal experience or sometimes by adopting the judgements that others have made about you. You can choose to reject or accept other people's descriptions of you depending on whether they fit your self-image.

If you have a positive self-image and someone comments that you have a big bum, it will not affect you in a negative way because either you will disagree with their comment or you know you have a big bum and you are OK with it.

However, if you have a negative self image and dislike your bum. When someone tells you that it looks big then you will feel really bad which will knock your confidence and in turn your self-esteem.

Sometimes when you don't like a particular part of yourself you tend to exaggerate that part of your body out of proportion. It becomes the focus every time you look in the mirror and you can start to forget that you have got some really great features that you do like. Try asking five people what they like about you physically; they might think of something that you have not thought of before. Write what they say below and discuss it with your coach.

Accepting yourself

Complete the table below using the headings to write in words or phrases that you believe describe you.

Try to be as positive as you can - if you are having difficulty imagine how someone else would describe you or use some of the comments from the previous page if you think they fit.

My physical appearance	
How I talk to other people	
My personality	

Look at the table and think of all the things about yourself that you cannot change, this could be the colour of your skin, your height, your shoe size, write them here:

Accept all these things because they are all part of you. Think back to the first part of the workbook and remind yourself of the physical challenges that you were good at. Write the things about your body that are cool, for example 'my legs are strong and I can kick a ball really hard'.

Now, go back over the list and highlight all the features you like and the things you believe are your strengths and positive qualities.

Now, in a different coloured highlighter do the same for all the things that you are not happy with.

For all the things that you were not happy with, think for a few minutes to try and determine what has influenced them. Write your thoughts in the box below.

What has influenced my negative self image?

Being optimistic and looking on the bright side

Do you think you are mostly a lucky or unlucky person? As a rule of thumb, if you think you are lucky then you will probably be quite optimistic, if you think you are unlucky then you will probably be quite pessimistic.

Putting a positive spin on things or looking on the bright side can generally make you feel better. Look at the table below, then fill in the blank spaces.

Optimism versus pessimism

Statement	Optimistic outlook	Pessimistic outlook
I am going for an interview on Thursday at College for a place on a nursery nurse course.	I am going to dress smartly and make sure that I come across as confident. I am likely to get a place because they will be able to tell that I really want to be a nursery nurse.	I always go to pieces when I'm nervous and they will think I am ridiculous. They will never give me a place because there will be loads of people there that come across better than me.
I am going ask that girl out that I have fancied for ages.	She might just say yes. I'm going to wear my best clothes and aftershave to help me to feel confident. If she says no it's her bad luck she won't know what she is missing.	She will probably say no, I don't even know why I'm trying. She is way out of my league. She will be laughing at me with all her mates and then I will feel really stupid.
I have a maths test tomorrow.		
I have a big spot right in the middle of my cheek.		

The power of language

It's very important that the way we use language in everyday situations is positive and healthy. It's not just the words we choose but the way we say them and the meaning we place on them. Think about different types of positive and negative language and complete the table below.

Positive language	Negative language
Giving compliments	Calling people names
Making mistakes is OK	Putting other people down
Friendly words	Criticising yourself or others

Now let's think about the impact of positive and negative words. Read the list of words below and discuss with your coach how they could influence your own self-worth and the self-worth of others. Decide if the words are positive or negative and write them in the column you feel they belong.

failure	selfish	useless	lazy
different	helpful	happy	open
strength	hopeless	power	enthusiastic
forgetful	organised	average	OK
responsible	aware	respect	dumb
jealousy	weak	fair	

Positive words	Negative words

How does our choice of language and words affect our self image and relationships?

Now that we have explored words and language, think about a time when you have used negative words and language and the same for positive words and language, discuss what effect both had.
This could be 'self talk', or communication directed at someone else, write about each below.

Negative

Positive

Concentrating on using positive words and language can help you feel happier. When you focus on the good and positive things about yourself and others, it can help you to feel optimistic and always look on the bright side. Even if you know you might not get that place on the football team at least you know you are going to give it your best shot and you are going to do everything possible to ensure you are performing at your best for your try out.

Developing self-esteem and confidence

There are many ways you can develop self-esteem and confidence. In some ways it can be like riding a bike, the more you practise the better you will become, even if you fall off or face set-backs you have to get back on and keep peddling. You have already started by doing the tasks in this section.

You can increase your self-esteem and confidence by choosing to do some form of exercise. By participating in exercise, whether it be going to the gym or going out for a run, can help you feel good about yourself. During exercise you set yourself realistic targets that you are able to achieve so you get a sense of accomplishment. For instance if you are a beginner, then you might set yourself the target of walking a mile, this is realistic and you can definitely achieve it. Exercise instructs your brain to release chemicals called endorphins into the body which give you a natural high and makes you feel good. As your exercise progresses and you set higher and higher targets your confidence soon begins to increase as you realise how far you have progressed and what potential you hold.

What sort of exercise do you do?

Is there any exercise you would like to try, if so what can you do about it?

What do you do to take care of yourself?

Looking after yourself can mean lots of different things. It can be stuff like keeping your body, hair and teeth clean, eating healthily, getting enough sleep or sharing your feelings with someone. When you look after yourself you can really enjoy the fun things in life and you can feel more able to face the difficult challenges. Try to think of as many different ways you look after yourself and write them below...

Helping yourself

Now, imagine that you have had a really busy day and you are feeling tired and stressed. What could you do to help yourself feel relaxed?

Ask three other people what they like doing to help themselves feel relaxed and write down what they say below.

Do you do lots of things to take care of yourself?

How do you treat yourself?

Would you treat a friend like you treat yourself?

Are there any changes you could make that would help you to take care of yourself better? If so what are they?

Setting goals

Just like the targets that you set yourself during exercise it is important to set yourself some goals in life. It's good to start small with short term targets like keeping your room tidy each week, or completing a piece of homework early. If you don't achieve every target, don't give yourself a hard time just set another one. Once you begin to achieve the small targets you can begin to build up to bigger ones.

Try to think of at least one short-term goal you could set yourself and write it below. Check out with your coach in your next session to see if you achieved your goal.

Setting destinations

Just like setting goals it's also good to set destinations. Think about times when you go out in a car with an adult. You tend always to be driving to a destination, it's not often you hear about people just driving round for the sake of it. If you set yourself a destination then it gives you something to work towards and focus on. For example if you decide that you want to play on a football team then you can work really hard during training to increase your chances of getting picked to play on the team. Or if you know that you want to be a nursery nurse then you can work towards ensuring that you get a college placement. When you know where it is that you are going, it can give you a strong sense of determination that drives you to get there. This will help when you are faced with challenges along the way and, once you have begun to overcome challenges, you will soon become resilient and learn the ability to bounce back.

Try to think of destinations that you might like to get to. Be realistic but try not to limit yourself, write them below.

Risk

All people take risks and it is a healthy and normal part of life. Different people perceive different things as being a risk. Some people struggle to take any risks and others don't seem to hold back on risks at all.

Taking risks is something that we all must do to develop, but there needs to be a balance. Some risks can have lasting effects and even endanger our lives.

Look at the table below suggesting healthy and unhealthy risks and add in any of your own.

Healthy risk	Unhealthy risk
• Join a club • Learn a language • Try your best • Take up a sport • Join a gym • Sign up for a race • Go hiking • Make a new friend	• Binge drinking • Taking drugs • Smoking • Unprotected sex • Being isolated • Having an account on social networking sites that is available for all to see

Discuss with your coach what you think the risks are around each point in the table.

Praise

Praise is part of positive language. When someone has done something really well or tried really hard they may be praised for it. Sometimes getting praise can make you feel very good about yourself. For some people when you are not used to getting praise it can feel a bit strange to receive it.

When someone praises you, how do you feel?

When was the last time you received praise, and what was it for?

Think of something you would like to be praised for?

Think of the last time you praised someone?

Think of ways you can praise other people?

Sometimes it can be good to praise yourself, this could be a bit like giving yourself a small reward for doing well, trying hard, or feeling proud of yourself. It's important to notice these things and not let them pass by without recognition. These small things can help to make you feel good every day. You could reward yourself for trying your best in your least favourite lesson.

Think of something you can praise yourself for and how you can praise or reward yourself, write it down here...

Compliments

Giving compliments is a bit like giving praise. Giving someone a compliment does two things, firstly it makes you feel good because it's a random act of kindness and secondly the person that you gave the compliment to feels good because you cared enough to notice. Giving yourself a compliment is about valuing yourself, recognising when you feel proud about something you have done or how you look.

Think of the last time you received a compliment and what was it for?

How did that compliment make you feel?

How did you take the compliment?

When was the last time you gave someone a compliment?

When was the last time you gave yourself a compliment?

You might be wondering about the last question but giving yourself a specific compliment can help you to focus on the good things you do and the great qualities you have. Think of something that you have done recently or look back at the 'positive qualities' work if you completed the section 'my feelings' and write yourself a specific compliment...

Homework task

Practise at giving yourself compliments and praise. It will probably be tricky to do and feel a bit weird if you're not used to it. At first it can be difficult to notice times when you deserve a compliment but the more you practise the more natural it will become. Try catching yourself feeling confident or good about something, you can do this at any time of the day in any situation so do your best and we will review how you are doing over the next couple of weeks...

Keep a diary or write things down so you don't forget, remember to bring it in to each session so you can show your coach the good work you have been doing.

Remember the diagram below when practising

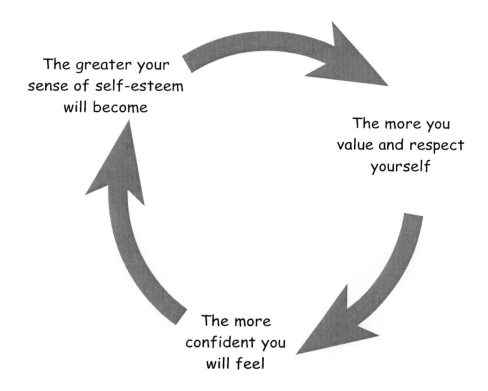

The greater your sense of self-esteem will become

The more you value and respect yourself

The more confident you will feel

Every time you do something towards respecting and valuing yourself you are boosting your confidence and raising your self-esteem.

Time to think

Now is your chance to think a bit more about the work you have just done about your confidence and self-esteem.

Here are a few questions to get you going:

- What three things have surprised you most?

- What did you already know?

- What three things are you most proud of?

- Is there anything you would like to do more of or change?

Use this page creatively to express your self-esteem!

Write a poem, draw, doodle – whatever you like.

Summary

Summary of my personal development workbook

In this workbook you have covered:

- All about ME
- My feelings
- My behaviour
- My relationships
- My self-esteem and confidence

It's now time to look back over all of the hard work you have done and summarise what you have learnt in each section.

All about ME

Look through the entire section with your coach. What are the main things you have learnt about yourself during this section?

What bits do you remember most?

All about ME

My feelings

Look through the entire section with your coach. What are the main things you have learnt in this section?

What bits do you remember most?

My behaviour

Look through the entire section with your coach. What are the main things you have learnt in this section?

What bits do you remember most?

My behaviour

My relationships

Look through the entire section with your coach. What are the main things you have learnt in this section?

What bits do you remember most?

My relationships

My self-esteem and confidence

Look through the entire section with your coach. What are the main things you have learnt in this section?

What bits do remember most?

My self-esteem and confidence

Overall

What skills have you developed during the workbook?

Tick all the ones you feel you have developed:

- ❑ Increased positive thinking

- ❑ Ability to respect other people

- ❑ Supporting yourself appropriately

- ❑ Improved communication with others

- ❑ Able to express feelings more appropriately

- ❑ Improved relationships

- ❑ Raised self-awareness

- ❑ Raised self-esteem

- ❑ Increased positive attitude towards yourself

- ❑ Ability to review and evaluate the values you hold

- ❑ Ability to take responsibility for your own life

- ❑ Ability to reflect on how your actions are influenced by your values, attitudes and past experiences

Moving on

Now that you have completed *My Personal Development Workbook* you can choose to move on to 'life story' work. Life story is collecting information about your past right from the moment you were born to give you a greater understanding of where you come from and what has happened to you. You may have done some life story work already. We can continue to build on this or we can start again from scratch. Life story work can be emotional and collecting information from your past can sometimes cause uncomfortable feelings. After completing this workbook you are better equipped to deal with this kind of stuff. So, if you feel you are ready and life story work is something that you want to do, you and your coach can discuss things and decide on how to take life story work forward. Some of the work you have completed in your workbook can be included as part of your life story.